IIIII I IIIIIIIIIIIII IIIIIII IIII
I0160453

*Advance Praise for*

# Igniting the Sacred Fire
## ~ Reinventing Yourself at Any Age ~

*"Igniting the Sacred Fire~Reinventing Yourself at Any Age* is a story of transformation, inspiration, re-invention, courage, and trust, ripped from the pages of author Adrianna Larkin's life and woven into a powerful, easy-to-read-and-comprehend manual for life."

~ Joe Rumbolo, radio host, "Healing the Universe: THE CLEAR VIBRATION"

*"Igniting the Sacred Fire ~ Reinventing Yourself at Any Age* goes straight to the heart of the flame and redefines the essential process of personal transformation. You'll have a new appreciation for all of your experiences and a new way to leverage them for a bright future!"

~ Lynn Scheurell, Creative Catalyst

"An inspirational read based on one woman's journey to inner strength, a destination where she discovers how to love and find acceptance for herself. This woman, Adrianna Larkin, shares her insights and secrets of how anyone can find their own sacred fire through personal journey and discoveries. A book that not only dares to inspire you but also teaches ways to challenge yourself for creating a better you."

~ Carrie Paradine, founder of www.tripleheartonline.com

"How would it be to live without the stories our ego made up to keep us from becoming fully, triumphantly ourselves? Adrianna Larkin shares her journey out of living a wouldacouldashoulda life into living the life her soul always wanted her to live. If she can do it, so can you. See yourself in her place as you read her book and envision yourself creating your own happy ending. I had chills reading the final page; her journey had, indeed, become my journey. Brava, Adrianna!"

Sheryl Lynn, radio host and author of
*Nine Roses for Chelsea: a Spiritual Journey*


"Adrianna Larkin is a beautiful and powerful word painter through her written and musical works. With the creativity of her multiple gifts and talents, she transforms us from a blank canvas to a brilliant masterpiece. She ignites unlimited possibilities that our heart and soul long to see, feel, and experience. As she ignites the scared fire within each one of us, we begin our own transformations. She is setting the world on fire, one spark at a time."

~ Jacque Weiss, Enrichment Expert


"Adrianna Larkin has done it again! *Igniting the Sacred Fire~Reinventing Yourself at Any Age* is just as inspirational as her music! After sharing our journeys of personal growth for years, it is very exciting to see our conclusions documented in her new book. This story could be anyone's life—with the ups and downs of Life School human experience. However, Adrianna takes this to another level with her unwavering search for meaning and the insightful results that she shares in powerful exercises and explanations for everyone to learn."

~ Susan Wright, founder of Tranquil Hearts

"Like most people I bristle at the thought that I could have attracted the negative circumstances in my life or that they are perfect for me — that 'I had a disproportionate number of wicked stepmothers, all with one kind of poison apple or another,' as Adrianna Larkin writes in *Igniting the Sacred Fire~Reinventing Yourself at Any Age*. After all, avoiding pain and seeking pleasure motivates human beings to change — *or so I thought…*

Often we need only turn on a light to see what is right in front of us — in the darkness. Connecting with our sacred fire can be as simple as flipping a switch — or as difficult as continually fumbling to find it. After a decade buried under an extra seventy pounds, I had compromised my health and extinguished all the fire in me — sacred or otherwise. Miserable and suffocating under my own girth, I thought nothing good could ever come from such hell. But I was wrong. Had I not been obese, I would never have sought medical treatment. And, *coincidentally*, the doctor who helped me saved the life of my only son (and from a hundred miles away) when his own doctors thought he would not recover. That poison apple — being overweight — caused the miracle and reignited my sacred fire. Now a size two, I have written two books and my son is healthy and back at Princeton.

*Igniting the Sacred Fire* pulses with a special courage rarely seen today, reaching readers at all levels of spiritual development, from the neophyte to those jaded along the walk of days. After suffering intense loss, Adrianna Larkin reclaimed her sacred fire and, with a generosity of spirit evident in her new book, illuminates the way for the rest of us. Her profound story offers the tools to lead others out of the dark cave of modern despair that smothers hope and stifles the spirit.

Am I happy I've been pelted by so many poison apples? Of course not. But now I see the *reason*: they didn't poison my life — they served as the impetus for change when I wouldn't listen any other way…and handed me a miracle.

I don't waste my poison apples anymore."

~ Cheryl Roberts, Ph.D.

"Wow. Adrianna Larkin offers a magical journey that takes you on an incredibly spiritual ride. With every challenge that she experienced, she created remarkable and empowering growth. I found this book to be truly inspirational and a *must read*. I love this book."

~ Gina Julie, radio host of "Empowering You"

"As I read Adrianna's book, I remember the many conversations we have had and appreciate the inspiration she has been to me as we have both been on our quest for spiritual growth and discovery of our true path and purpose. This book is a tool for others to receive the same inspiration and encouragement I have experienced through her thoughts and wisdom. I have watched as Adrianna reinvented herself; and her story gives all of us the knowing that we can follow our bliss – at any age!"

~ Diann Robins

"I believe people are brought into our lives for a reason. I met Adrianna many years ago and we had such a connection – music, both wanting to be authors, owning our own business. After reading her book, I realize we have one more thing in common—wanting to help people to spark a fire. This book provides some wonderful real life examples that just connect with the reader. And once they connect, they don't let go."

~ Dawn Mushill, author of *Customer Service and Beyond*

"Adrianna Larkin's *Igniting the Sacred Fire* is written with vulnerability and courage, inviting us on a compelling journey of discovery. Her insight, experience, and compassion fill the pages, all the while tugging at heartstrings and humor to remind us of our own amazing possibilities. It's a journey some may be hesitant to begin—but I'll be always grateful that I did."

~ Jenna Garrett, WordWorks, writer and editor

"How do I get from where I am to where I want to be?" That's how Adrianna Larkin poses the question that is near, and perhaps not so dear, to everyone's heart. *Igniting the Sacred Fire* is delightfully written and frighteningly candid as it tells a story and provides a map—not *the* map, but *a* map—for challenging fear and using it as a springboard for reinventing oneself. It is poignant and humorous and shares a tale we are all interested in—because it's everyone's story."

~ Bruce McLaughlin, Ed.D
Career & Transition Coach and author of *The Jesus Affirmations: Using Biblically-Based Truths to Develop Healthy Habits of Mind*

"What a breath of fresh air Adrianna's book is. Not only is it an effortless, delightful read, it relates to everyone—whether you've been forced to reinvent yourself in the past or you are facing it for the first time. Whether you've been around the block before or you're making your first lap, **Sacred Fire** is filled with inventive and thoughtful insight. It comes highly recommended—from someone who's been around the block a few times."

~Michael "Supe" Granda, Bassist
The Ozark Mountain Daredevils

"The youngest, whitest, Native American Wisdom Keeper, 'Little Grandmother,' said that it is now time for us to 'get it.' She refers to the urgent need for us to wake up to our power, our magnificence, and potential. In **Igniting the Sacred Fire ~ Reinventing Yourself at Any Age**, Adrianna Larkin places a light along the path of doing precisely that."

~ Bob Keeton
Living Successfully, LLC

# Igniting the Sacred Fire

## ~ Reinventing Yourself at Any Age ~

# Also from Adrianna Larkin

*Transformation, Essays on Love, Healing and Water*
An anthology of essays by fifteen contributing writers
Soul Based Living Books

*Sacred Fire: A Journey of Transformation (E-book)\**
The story behind the music

❧

*Original Music*
CDs currently available

*Sacred Fire*
*Signs of the Times\*\**
*Coming Home*
*No Ingenue*

All are available through www.adriannalarkin.com
\*\*Also available through www.wildoatsrecords.com
\*Free Download

# Igniting the Sacred Fire

## Reinventing Yourself at Any Age

## Adrianna Larkin

**MP** Minan Publishing

Published by Minan Publishing

Copyright © 2009 by Adrianna Larkin

All rights reserved.

No part of this book may be reproduced or transmitted in any form or by
any means, electronic or mechanical, including photocopying, recording or by
an information storage and retrieval system, without permission in writing
from the author, except where prohibited by law.

This book was not designed to provide medical advice, professional
diagnosis, or treatment services in any form to the reader. The author
presents her views as general information for educational purposes only and
these are not to be used as a substitute for professional care. The author
disclaims any liability arriving directly or indirectly from the use of this book,
or any subject matter offered within.

Cover design by Lauren Stewart
Cover Photography licensed from dreamstime.com
Background photography: Patrick Hajzler

First edition printed in the United States of America

ISBN: 978-0-9844807-0-8

First printing 2010

For permission to use selections from this book contact:
Minan Publishing
P.O. Box 181
Troy, IL 62294

*For my husband Michael,*
*whose reflection returns to me*
*as my own beauty.*

# Table of Contents

# Foreword

The ability to change is truly one of the most difficult challenges we face in our third dimensional world, with a scientific foundation born of our basic DNA code and simple human resistance to move into the unknown.

In her most recent book, *"Igniting the Sacred Fire,"* Adrianna Larkin has created a compelling story of change and transition, approaching the topic not only from the mind but from the heart. So often this genre attempts to tell you what to do, outlining specific rules and practices. Not so in this case. Through question, invitation, and example, Adrianna helps you see yourself in a new light, peeling off the layers of worn-out thoughts and behavior — allowing you to see the familiar not as you *thought* it was but as it truly is.

You will be swept away by the story and forced to take pause while you examine your own journey. And one of the greatest takeaways here is the understanding that your change and transformation may come at any time, at any age.

This story will help you remove your own limitations and fear-based beliefs. Those fears will be replaced with hope and wonder and the joy of expectation. You will remember what you felt like as a child — when the world held so many possibilities.

It was to my great benefit that I booked passage on Adrianna's journey, and I know you'll enjoy the ride as much as I did. Be sure to take your time to drink it all in. This is not a quick read or a fantasy — but truly a story of hope and enlightenment.

~ Joe Nunziata, author of *Spiritual Selling*

Igniting the Sacred Fire

# Acknowledgements

*To my husband Michael*, whose Herculean support helped make this book a physical reality.

*To our children — Matt, Dave, and Michelle —* who remain my most consistent teachers.

*To Gloria Horrell*, who extended beyond her role as editor to become cheerleader, creative consultant, and layout artist.

*To Lauren Stewart*, whose dedication to the graphic presentation of this piece made the cover that much more stunning.

*To those friends* whose loving energy lighted my way in the darkest times and who I could not even begin to name in either order of appearance or importance…so I will defer to the alphabet once again:

*Dave Black*, for his unwavering grace and professional skill as a friend and musician.

*Al Diaz*, for his understanding and support for the greater calling of a literary muse.

*Janice Gregory*, for her friendship, support, and daily pep talks — as well as her remarkable talents as "publicist extraordinaire."

*Tom Maloney*, for his never-ending flow of unsolicited support and encouragement.

*Joe Nunziata*, for his talent, wisdom, and dedication in crafting the foreword for this book.

*Diann Robins*, whose channel of wisdom has proven invaluable and helped make this book more than a dream.

*Joe Rumbolo*, a true "tower of power" in his steadfastness as friend and mastermind partner.

*Benet Schaeffer*, for his shared gift of insight and impeccably keen sense of *right timing*.

*Jacque Weiss*, whose friendship, love, light, and sisterhood chose to join me on this journey of self-evolution.

*Mae Wheeler*, who continues to share her wise counsel and mentoring…may I always be a worthy disciple.

*Susan Wright*, whose unyielding push to bring me into the light (or perhaps drag me there) is finally paying off.

*And to my parents, Velma and Mitchell Frutko*, as well as all of my other teachers past, present, and future—both known and unknown—who continue to light my way in this world and all others…

I am grateful.

# Introduction

## "You Are Here" — This is Why

Since I have a sense of direction that is nearly legendary in its ability to leave me lost or turned around, I learned early on to compensate by using a map. I began my apprenticeship with the maps in the mall as a teenager, finding them easy to use because they always had that little arrow pointing to my exact location, telling me: "You are here." And if someone knows where I am, I'm not lost at all.

Knowing where you are should never be underestimated in any activity. It is the key ingredient to remaining in the present moment and the orientation we need before setting out on any journey. It is only after we understand where we are that we can figure out in which direction we are traveling and determine if we are closer to, or further away from, our desired destination.

Most people who find themselves "here" in this book fall into one of two categories:

1. They have suffered a personal crisis such as a health issue, divorce, layoff, foreclosure, bankruptcy, (or something just as significant to them), creating a feeling of substantial loss, or...
2. They are experiencing a restlessness of some kind, suggesting their life should be different. And while they may not know in what way, or how to go about making the change, this restlessness is causing them to question everything that they once knew as being comfortable or important.

There is a third category of people who might find themselves here as well. They may not feel a strong desire to reinvent themselves at this time, or perhaps they've chosen to do just that and have found the way to do so. Still, they are curious—and wish to know what can be found among these pages, whether it is simple validation or some comfort in knowing they aren't the only one.

Before we go any further, I should tell you: I am not a psychologist, a therapist, a life coach or an expert in any area of self help. I am, however, someone who birthed this process—every single step of it—from *all* of the crises named in the first category, while living with the restlessness described in the second.

It was the third state—that of curiosity—that served as the midwife for this process and watched it grow up to be a book. I wanted to know if I could take what I had parented as my own method, and offer it as something beneficial for others. This third, small, but very important thread is what brought me to this point. It is also the spark of my current sacred fire.

So I am now *here* too, right along with you.

Whatever may be the case for your arriving here, I am glad you came. If you fall into the first or second group of people mentioned earlier, you are about to embark on an amazing journey. I hope you can trust the discomfort that brought you *here* is serving as a threshold to something wonderful and magnificent: the <u>you</u> of your desires. How do I know? Because you have begun the search...which brings us to the "why" part of "you are here."

And since we are both staring at that same little arrow now, I need to say: I am only one voice, a single selection from the smorgasbord of many truths and teachers that are here to serve you on your journey. My own process was pieced together from what I learned from them, so I'll be introducing you to many of them along the way.

Just as there are many truths, there are a number of universal myths still lurking in the area of growth and personal development. In my opinion they do more harm than good, so I would like to give them brief mention and explain that they will *not* be found among these pages.

**Myth #1: You will always be able to remain in your comfort zone as you travel your path to personal growth.**

Any teacher I have ever considered to be of value, at some point made me more than a little uncomfortable. It is, as humans, simply how we grow. Questioning, wondering — even looking for answers among these pages — would most likely never have happened if you were completely comfortable where you are.

It is interesting to me that, as children, we do not let the fear of discomfort become a barrier to mastery. I remember watching my son learn to walk. I can't remember how many times he lost his balance and fell. I do, however, remember one fall that resulted in a trip to the emergency room — and two stitches — when his chin made perfect contact with the corner of the wall. That did not stop him. He immediately returned to exploring his world again. It is beyond comprehension to imagine that any toddler would experience their first fall and say, "You know what? I can't do this, it's too hard. I'm only going to crawl from now on."

Once upon a time this world of ours seemed like a wonderful place to discover. The truth? It still is. Anything that you made an effort to learn or experience for the first time—whether it was walking, riding your bike, your first kiss or the tasks of your first job—came with no knowledge, no experience, a lot of mistakes, and more than a healthy dose of challenges...physical, mental, *and* emotional.

Stop and think what happened when you finally succeeded. How good did it feel when you got your driver's license, learned to dance, could play a piece of music, or execute a football play? What kind of feeling washed over you as you realized your accomplishment of what once seemed alien to you? Were the steps you took to get there always easy? Were they comfortable? My guess is they were not.

This won't be either. Moving outside of our comfort zone, to try new things and re-engage with childlike wonder, is a test of mastery that we will have again and again.

**Myth #2: There is only one real truth and I am the only teacher or announcer of this truth. Once you have it, there is no need of anything else.**

Any teacher or process that declares to have all the answers usually has very few, if any. After an experience with my own misplaced faith, I now understand: fear is the source of a great insecurity, which feels that it must have complete loyalty in order to have strength. The truth is that anything of real substance can always bear scrutiny, or be supported by other truths. Good teachers invite questions.

I once had a friend who was an ordained clergyman. As a very good friend, we had known each other for a number of years. Before he was ordained—and even after—my husband and I would often have dinner, go dancing, and attend a number of social events with him and his wife.

He made the comment one day that he would be devastated if his daughter ever expressed a desire to even *visit* a church of another faith, considering it a slight to his own. At that time, I didn't have the heart to challenge him on the statement this made about his own ability to 1.) imprint the goodness of his faith on his offspring, 2.) trust that his religion would not be seen as inferior to another, or 3.) have his faith and truth supported by another doctrine.

Although it is not my nature to make blanket statements, I'm going to go out on a limb here and offer that any teaching of value does not need to declare itself as the only right one. Any teaching of value makes a case for us all being connected and allowing our diversity to exist harmoniously and without judgment. Any teaching of value takes the wisdom from many teachings and thus can be found in other sources.

**Myth #3: Once I get—or learn to manifest—what I want, I will be happy.**

You would have to look hard to find a bigger fan of the movie "The Secret" when it was first released. I thought it was a beautifully produced work with marvelous graphics. It offered an all-star cast of speakers, authors, and experts in personal and spiritual growth. It moved many, including myself, to become acquainted with an expanded range of information and resources.

It has been noted, however, by non-fans and spiritual teachers alike, that in the final edit the message that was communicated led many people to believe they only need visualize or think about what they desire in order to master the Law of Attraction. After they get what they want, they can then be happy.

Happiness from any external source, such as the acquisition of a house, a car, a new job or the perfect relationship, is temporary at best. The newness of a house or car has a limited lifespan, as does the next job or a "perfect" relationship if you have not done the work *internally*.

More exploration of spiritual law reveals that it is an *already existing* state of happiness that is the primary factor in acquiring what you want with the greatest amount of ease.

## What's Next?

Now that we have established "we are here" and know where we are going (without the detours or roadblocks offered by common myths) you should know what happens next.

If I have done my job correctly, being uncomfortable may be something you could learn to be slightly comfortable with—and personal growth will not end with this book, but move you to seek the source of this information. You may find an increased desire to become more acquainted with the many teachers and truths that are mentioned here, or find your own. Your present circumstance will spark the fire that becomes your true purpose, and in that purpose a renewed happiness or a self-assurance you did not have previously starts to emerge. What shows up as the byproduct of that purpose and happiness will be breathtaking, if not seemingly miraculous.

A trip of any kind holds the potential for limitless adventure, and I hope you're looking forward to this journey as much as I am.

# Prologue

## A Lesson in Love

*"On a full moon night with a far off stare,*
*from cool gray eyes that remain aware*
*of all the demons that still surround him there, he stands just as before..."*
*...from Man O'War, song lyrics*
*- Adrianna Larkin -*

The service had been carried out according to my father's wishes—almost. In all likelihood he would have objected to having any service at all, which is why he had insisted on cremation..."so that no one feels like they have to visit my grave and cry over me." But my mother needed that cry. And he wasn't in charge anymore.

As for me, I was pretty sure that the emotion that filled me wasn't grief as much as it was anger. The years of resentment, frustration, and betrayal I felt didn't translate to tears. Just rage. Because of him I was trapped in a job that left me drained, exhausted, with no way out; and now I would never have a chance to tell him.

There was a good deal left unsaid at the time of his death—things that never *could* be said because he was so sick. My dad was a free spirit; he had lived apart from us as much as he lived with us. In my mind, he had controlled my life and pummeled every effort I had made to lay claim to the same spirited life he chose to live with abandon.

It was about two months later when the rest of the details were addressed and life was starting to feel normal again that Dad staged a visit in a lucid dream. He was behind the wheel of an old car I used to have that was standing still in traffic, seeming to represent the presence of other souls who were having conversations with loved ones. He smiled, and as I reached over to hug him I could feel the stubble of his beard and the fabric of his shirt against my skin. "Get in Honey, we need to talk."

His words were perfectly clear, but his lips weren't moving. And ready to fault find as I was, I told him in no uncertain terms how much his telepathic communication "creeped me out." He chuckled with another telepathic response: "You'll get used to it—get in."

"You *are* dead, right?" I asked.

"Yep...as a doornail," he replied. His face was radiant, as robust and healthy as he had appeared before the disease. He flashed that toothy Cheshire Cat grin I knew I had inherited from him...the one that only showed itself when we were completely elated (or extremely pleased with ourselves).

"And I assume since you're smiling you're in a *good place*?" I asked.

"A very good place, a beautiful place...that's partly what I came to tell you."

I could sense around him even more peace than he had engendered in physical form. But my curiosity got the better of me. "If you feel all that peace, why would you come to me now—I mean, don't you surrender your 'earthly cares' and all that jazz?"

I had to ask. The man *was* dead. And while it felt very strange—and good—to have this time with him, I couldn't see why he would be so bent on visiting me *now*.

"Yes, but the great thing...*the really wonderful thing*, is that you get to keep the love. In fact it is all that you really *do* keep. Everything that you are doing in this lifetime, all that you are and all you will become is sifted through at the end and what remains...is just love."

I felt like I'd fallen into a scene from *Ghost*; and I was about to say as much when he leaned in with those intense hazel eyes that I knew were about to make a point. "This is what you must always remember: while you have this time, take every opportunity to generate as much love as possible, fill your heart with it, be a catalyst for it, do good deeds, receive it and give it. It is what we all became human to experience, and it makes the afterlife so much sweeter. I loved you and your mother so much that I never wanted to see you suffer. There is something I would like to give you — to help you understand..."

At that point, in what would equate to a couple of hours of conversation in a physical time plane, I experienced a human "download" of his thoughts, feelings, motivation, fears, and insecurities—all born out of an intense love and concern for my well being that was colored by his own experience and the tragic life he lived.

What I realized was—given the same set of circumstances, the same feelings, the same experiences— loving my child as I did, *I would have likely acted in the exact same way.*

I sensed our time growing short; and he echoed this as he told me he would have to go soon. But my curiosity wasn't done with him yet. I asked why on earth (and he smiled at that turn of phrase) he had shown up behind the wheel of one of my old clunkers. He told me that because I had a fondness for this car in particular I would notice it immediately, and that would help me notice him. He had returned at his own choosing and wanted to allow me that same respect—a choice—knowing I could just as easily have rejected his invitation to receive him in this meeting place of souls.

"How 'bout it?" he asked. The smile had never left his face. "Traffic is starting to move again. Do you want to take this thing for a nostalgic spin before I go? You can drive."

His offer caught me by surprise.

"Daddy!" It was rare for me to call him that. Not since I had been a child had I used the title that represented this most precious term of endearment. "You know my driving always made you crazy!"

I recalled all the times he demonstrated his white-knuckle pose, with one hand on the dash and one holding the passenger handle which would allow him to either grip hard or bail as the situation called for. He did this well into his later years, up until the last time I saw him.

If possible, his grin became even larger now as he prepared to deliver the greatest line of all time.

"Yeah...but I figure it's different this time."

And he paused for the full effect.

"You can't kill a *dead* man."

That's when I awakened. I was sitting straight up in bed, tears rolling down my face, laughing out loud and crying at the same time.

But now—finally—I understood.

# Chapter One

### Genesis

*"I have a story, you can read between the lines*
*for the power and the glory found in once upon a time,*
*With lives like tapestries so colorful and fine, they weave their way home..."*
*...from* I Have a Story, *song lyrics*
*- Adrianna Larkin -*

My own sacred fire was ignited the summer of 2007. This is the beginning of that story...

The line from a Gordon Lightfoot song was now a loop that played over and over again in my brain. It had long since separated itself from the song to dominate my thoughts. Gradually it began filling the space usually occupied by accounting, ordering, production, and other details of the custom frame shop and art gallery I owned with my husband.

The weather was amazing for this time of year. On an unseasonably cool summer day, it allowed for the sun to be invited rather than avoided. I turned up the volume on the CD player in the car and rolled the windows down. The breeze felt good in my hair. The day's sense of freedom was beyond what I usually felt on my way to see a commercial client, and Lightfoot was the perfect backdrop for this ride. His music always awakened a sort of wanderlust in me—it brought back good memories.

It had been awhile since I felt like this.

I was taking every opportunity to do site visits at commercial locations, as it got me out of the shop and provided a welcome relief from addressing the issues of wrong materials, accounts payable, and endless phone calls. It also instilled a sense of control in fostering increased sales without waiting for the customers to come to us. A complimentary walk-through offered the chance of writing a proposal, and I was pursuing all prospects to boost our revenue. Our survival depended on it.

The weight of owning a small business seemed like a fair trade for a career that allowed me to interact with the arts. In our small shop of less than 700 square feet, we found a way to host events featuring live music, children's programs, and many of the elements that fueled my creative fires. These events not only offered a good marketing strategy for exposure but they also returned something critical to me that I missed in leaving my own art form behind.

The past couple of days had made it easier. Even though we were busy at the shop, I had managed to slip out for a lunch with my film-making friend Susan. Since that meeting two days ago, I had felt infused with this strange kind of energy surrounding her project. She was planning her first full-length feature film. As she explained her concept and shared the plans she had for original music, I could feel a return of the long-lost electricity that used to freely move over my skin with a creative venture. Some of it remained with me as I basked in the sunshine and music of my youth.

My meeting with Susan had been for both business and pleasure. She had used some of my earlier original music in her recently produced "short" films; so I was not surprised when she shared the outline of her new project about baby boomers and asked me to compose the music for it. I didn't need time to think about it, I simply agreed. Time constraints were not even a consideration. She was a great friend and I wanted to support her. I always felt she had a big part to play in my own career development, so we talked some more.

She was fine with using some of the other songs I had created—the ones she had not used in previous projects. There were a number of those to choose from, at least 40 or so. God knows I wasn't doing anything with them. I had offered—and she agreed—that a few of the key scenes needed songs crafted specifically for them.

And something special had to be created for the climax: that pivotal moment when the main characters—after so much struggle—gain the insight *and* the juice they need to recreate their lives.

The electricity was becoming stronger just thinking about our conversation. It was nice to be able to revisit the side of me that could express itself this way. Something else was coming through my thoughts, however: my own lyric thread was starting to emerge and I felt a sense of urgency to capture it before the words went away. I had learned a long time ago not to trust that a great inspiration could be reclaimed when it was convenient. I looked around in search of something in the car to take notes on. My planner was in the back seat.

The voice recorder I kept under the seat for these kinds of situations had long since broken and I had never replaced it. Before buying it, some of my best songs had been written on napkins, fast food bags, and any scrap of paper found inside the car. Shuffling the few things on the seat next to me, I found an envelope and scribbled something on the back. Since I could not pull over and had to keep my eyes on the road, I trusted my hand would just go where it needed to and that I could decipher it later.

This was a familiar pattern and the genesis for my music: the words appeared first. Occasionally, the start of a melody would begin the song, but most often I wrote lyrics—a leftover from my days of writing poetry and short stories as a teenager. The melody that showed up to join the words would be developed to best support the mood of the lyrics. Rhythm and phrasing would be fine-tuned in the production stage for the maximum effect.

After getting it started, it seemed like the song I was inspired to write would write itself. I would often look at what I had written and watch as the words seemed to relocate themselves on the paper in front of me. At times it seemed like I was in an altered state—at the very least a *Harry Potter* movie. I would look down and have words appear that I could not remember writing, and yet know that they were the warp and weave of the song's intent.

I felt a true sense of power in Susan's project, and my marketing mind knew that it was timely. It would appeal to a massive demographic, graced with the skill Susan brought to the table as an excellent script writer. I felt certain she would be picked up at a major film festival. This piece had a powerful message...and coming from her teaching background, I counted on her to provide it as a lesson. It would be such a cool thing if some of my music could really bring that home.

What I remembered most about that day was the brief exchange in the parking lot as we left each other's company. She had paused after walking about ten feet toward her car. Looking over her shoulder, she spoke the words that transmuted the electricity on my skin to something internal that lodged itself in my spine.

Susan's eyes are one of her most remarkable features—they carry the light of compassion. Over time this compassion has become flavored with humor and wisdom that give her the appearance of an old soul—just one of the many reasons we had become friends. We had grown to know each other very well as we moved through our common experiences of home repairs, single parenting, and business ownership; and I was certain that I had seen every expression that could possibly reveal itself in those 15 years of shared history.

When she turned to speak as she did that day, I couldn't shake the thought of how different she looked. A new expression had altered the features of her face in a way I had never seen before. Even her tone of voice had changed and she sounded much younger—like a child speaking with innocence. It was as if she paused just long enough to let another being into her body and that entity was now speaking through her.

"Nan?"

I paused also, turning to take in the newness of this sound.

"Yes?" I replied.

"This *will* make you rich."

That was all she said. The new being-and-friend composite remained to make certain that the electricity on the surface of my skin was moving inward—then turned to get into her car.

I remembered the last time I felt this way, connecting it to the day I read the advertisement that began with "business for sale." It described a "turn-key" operation ready to be taken over. The owners were retiring and wished to sell.

I had told my husband Mike, "We need to check into this. I know we talked about waiting to go into business for ourselves until Michelle was out of college, but I have a feeling..."

That feeling was all that was needed. The word "cutback" was being tossed around at both of our places of employment. This word, along with my feeling, seemed to place a self-employment opportunity in a whole new light. We had already imagined the worst case scenario that would leave us both unemployed within the same 60 days.

Perhaps I was motivated, but I had learned to trust my instinct. It was good that I did. That feeling of electricity placed Mike and I ahead of our timetable to purchase a business within three years. It matched his skills with woodworking and carpentry to mine for marketing, customer service, and corporate relations. It aligned us with the one business that seemed like a perfect fit for us both. As an added bonus, we had a connection with the arts...a space that had been left empty — especially for me.

The prior owners were delightful people. They remained with us for 30 days after purchase to assist the transition. We felt a real kinship with them and they were patient teachers. My learning curve seemed off the charts as I experienced my first retail setting, learned the specifics of each vendor and supplier relationship, as well as design for custom framing.

Mike and I agreed that it made sense for him to

oversee production. I would take care of administration, accounting, and paperwork, which would put me in the shop during peak traffic times to wait on customers. I could be out of the shop early in the morning or later in the afternoon to market our services. That marketing paid off. After 18 months we had grown so much we had to make a choice: hire a part-time employee or cut back on marketing. It wasn't much of a choice. We hired an employee.

Another eight months in my role as a full-time marketing person and acting as a commercial interface caused Mike's production load to double. We made another choice to hire more help for the production area, and our growth now seemed explosive. I was beginning to understand what I did not know before: why small businesses face some of the most severe challenges in their growth phase. A fellow business owner provided further clarification—his knowledge and counsel were welcomed, the comparison: not so much.

"Do you know why many herbicides work?"

"No," I replied.

"They work because they force such a rapid growth in the weed it cannot be supported by the nutrients it needs to sustain it. It dies from starvation."

I remembered feeling slightly queasy with his analogy. It was a little *too* familiar. Increased production meant increased supplies and materials which meant more phone calls, mistakes in shipping, and fires to put out. Some days there simply wasn't enough of me to go around.

Then there was our space. With all four of us working in the back at the same time, it often felt like we spent most of our time tripping over each other. One account we acquired involved more than 50 pieces for us to frame and approximately four days in which to do it. The thought was tempting, but I quickly ruled out contacting my few artist friends with framing experience who could have shortened those 20-hour days. I had no place to put them.

I was feeling a lot like someone had sprinkled *our* shop with a poison. We had grown just enough to need more help, but not enough to commit to a larger space that would support and nourish the extra staff. Were we growing only to *die*? I had to get us to that critical next level. Just a bit more revenue and I could justify a bigger space...

I had long since turned off Gordon Lightfoot, but one line from the title track of *Don Quixote* remained in my head — the words that cautioned of those who sought to devour the life essence, so aptly termed "sacred fire."

Now I knew why it had stayed with me. This line of the song expressed exactly how I felt. Since taking over the shop, I had done battle with the village government over the sign ordinance to increase our visibility; I was still reeling from the multiplied expense of payroll taxes, worker's compensation, and unemployment insurance that came with hiring employees; I had undertaken this shop with the best of intentions, but everything that seemed sacred to me felt like it was being devoured.

Some days it was all I could do to sweep up the bones.

*Being self-employed is not for sissies,* I thought.

In meeting the demands of the shop I had all but given up on music and any songwriting efforts, thinking I had made peace with taking that train to the end of the tracks. It seemed like a good run. I had spent years pitching to publishers in hopes of getting a commercial release, but it never came. I recorded 3 CDs — one of them on an independent label in Nashville, hoping to capture the attention of their European market — that didn't happen. I had written a theme song for radio and even another for a television pilot that was canned before it could be completed. After 15 years of crafting music and performance around all my other jobs, there was no sign that I was any closer to success than when I started. I was almost 50 years old. It was time to let it go.

I was too flippin' old to be playing this game anymore.

Mike seemed to weather the business ups and downs better than I did; but then he wasn't being stalked by the same family history that was haunting me. I was a third generation business owner. My dad had built his business around selling sunglasses and souvenirs to gas stations; but when the energy crisis hit in the mid 70s, the traffic he depended on to support sales all but died. Those economic conditions had forced him to declare bankruptcy.

My grandfather owned a furniture store on the east coast during the depression. Rumor had it that he withstood the stock market crash much better than he did my grandmother's death from cancer. It was the combination of those two events that was more than he — or his business — could endure.

"Failure is not an option," I stated confidently to bankers and customers alike. I offered this even in spite of my growing fear of a family curse. I *thought* I knew what I was made of: I had the tenacity and I had the education. My prior experience as an emergency room nurse gave me a good sense of priorities. My corporate experience had honed my marketing skills.

But try as I might, I did not get a vision of Mike and I remaining in the shop long term.

It made no sense. We had done — and were still doing — amazing things. Mike's attention to detail and craftsmanship earned us a solid reputation. In addition to bringing in commercial accounts, we worked on new ways to service our residential clients. I sought input from our employees on customer service features. Both of them had come to us with retail management experience — something I did not have.

I took pride in the feeling that we were elevating industry standards. Within the first two years of purchasing the shop, we had made the front page cover of a primary trade magazine. As we created processes and programs, everything was considered in light of a possible franchise. I knew we were doing *everything* right.

Then why was I so afraid?

It could have been the sleep deprivation. I hadn't had a good night's sleep since we purchased our business three years earlier, and the fitful dreams and sleepless nights had become the status quo. In my attempt to make certain no stone was left unturned, I found it hard to shut down.

My thoughts went back to Susan. Creating a soundtrack for her film would be a great help to her. More than anything, it would be a great diversion for me. I could do something *fun* for a change. Something I would not normally do for myself.

Something *easy.*

# Chapter Two

## Another Voice

*"Another sleepless night
and I'm promised to the lyric dancing in my head,
While a melody winds like an infinite thread
that longs to be music played..."*
*...from* Music Played, *song lyrics*
*- Adrianna Larkin -*

I emptied the contents of my arms onto the kitchen counter. Among these items retrieved from the interior of the car was the note I had scrawled on the back of the envelope while driving: *It starts as a drum in the distance...*

I could actually decipher the handwriting I had entrusted to my sense of feel rather than my sense of sight. I let my eyes move over the line of words, calling up the thought stream I was having when I wrote them.

I envisioned that the climactic scene from Susan's film would require a powerful piece of music to serve as an anthem. The production of the music was especially important for that scene and would demand much more than a bare-bones guitar, although the guitar would furnish the underlying rhythm. Heavy drums coupled with percussion would drive the point home and give it real power.

My eyes returned to the paper to take in the other phrase I had crafted: *a rhythm of something so strong*...yes, the rhythm was important...and noticed there was a connection between the reference of rhythm and the first sentence that was suggestive of lyrics. They had actually lined up on the piece of paper in an unintended yet familiar way...in the way that only lyrics would line up for me.

How interesting that the words meant to serve only as descriptive notes for the music were taking on the appearance of lyrics. This was cool—and the electricity had now returned full force to rest on the surface of my skin. It was squashing the hint of guilt that threatened to emerge as the result of ignoring business e-mails, laundry, and all the other *normal* things that usually received my immediate attention upon returning home.

*And you do what you can to resist this, believing it must be all wrong.*

Now my heart was beating wildly as the natural rhythm of the words seemed to make itself known. I added this additional line and gave thanks, as I often do, in quiet gratitude to my Muse while waiting in that perfect space to receive the next gift of words.

*'Til the sound fills your head with your heartbeat.*

This was gonna be good. I remained there, with eyes closed, continuing my offering of appreciation as I waited patiently for the next precious gift to follow this one, but there was nothing. Sadly, I knew that was all for now. The inspiration — and electricity — left as quickly as it came.

I was disappointed, but I had long since learned that my Muse would come and go as it pleased...with or without invitation. I only understood it as a sort of abstract voice in my head. The Muse never had a physical form. It was gender neutral. I didn't know if it was short or tall, fat or skinny. It was simply energy. It could awaken me from a sound sleep in the middle of the night or appear in broad daylight. It wouldn't hesitate to interrupt as I spoke with a co-worker or member of my family, at which point I would have to excuse myself to "write something down" before I forgot.

I had become very adept over the years at living with what seemed like a split-screen effect, performing actions in the well known third dimension of my surroundings, as my mind would be called to another realm unknown to anyone but me.

I looked at the words again, now fully formed as three distinct lines which I read out loud:

*It starts as a drum in the distance, a rhythm of something so strong*
*And you do what you can to resist this, believing it must be all wrong*
*'Til the sound fills your head with your heartbeat...*

These words, these incredible words — they were delicious. No matter how many times I had offered myself to this process, it never ceased to amaze me. I had learned a long time ago that the best material was channeled. I could force it, but I would never be as pleased with the final outcome as much as if I just allowed it to happen.

I had no doubt that a higher power was working through me, and I took a moment to savor the complete awe of being a vehicle for this creation. I thought of my often-voiced reference to Genesis, but this song was more of the Gospel according to St. John:

"In the beginning was the Word."

The more serious side of this reverie faded as I allowed my imagination to hopscotch directly to a parody of the Bible. It was a quick descent to depravity as an impromptu skit starring two stoned flower children, sharing some "organic recreation" while reciting scripture, began to play as a movie in my head.

*"Hey Man...in the beginning, there was like...the WORD, man..."*

*"Yeah man, and the word was, like, with GOD..."*

That my mind could make the instant switch to something so irreverent would no doubt make me seem a little disrespectful in the eyes of many (myself included), but I felt confident God had a sense of humor. That was a good thing for me. I knew that my mind was much too far reaching to remain conventional for very long. Still, I felt assured that this comedic turn was not the *most* sacrilegious thought stream out there. In fact I was pretty certain that if I had to own a label, my packaging would read "Heretic Lite."

Since I was not receiving any further inspiration, I took it as a cue to return to my reality of the present moment. Although I wished I could have finished what had been started, I was accepting that I couldn't force the process. That did not mean, however, that I was too good to beg.

And while I didn't have any preconceived idea of what my Muse looked like, I often imagined that it was the Muse's secretary who served as my entry point to that higher realm. In my mind the secretary took on the guise of a gum popping, nail filing, disconnected receptionist with a high-pitched nasal voice. And that voice made my imagination's rendition of it even more annoying. I could not resist my hunger for more words however, as I appealed to this imaginary gatekeeper.

*"Please, give me more, I need **more**, I have to have the help of my Muse,"* I begged.

"I'm sorry, Ma'am, I don't know when your Muse will return." She seemed a little too smug in the delivery of this information.

My soul begged yet again, but it was obvious Muse's receptionist wasn't going to budge.

"No, Ma'am, I have no idea...that's right, I can't tell you." I could actually see her smiling now, as she continued to file her nails—her pleasure increasing in direct response to my frustration.

*What a witch,* I thought to myself. *She* does *know, she's just not telling.*

My imagination continued its mockery in that annoying nasal voice. "The Muse keeps very irregular hours."

*Tell me something I don't already know.* At that point I would have slammed down the phone—had I been holding one—and finding that I had spoken out loud made me glad no one was around to hear me.

I was supposed to meet with Susan the next day, and I was eager to show her more—I *had* to produce more. We were on a timeline. My corporate and now business mind had put me on a production schedule, but nothing had come in since a couple of days ago when I wrote the lines that seemed to form themselves from my thoughts.

Having cleared my calendar and making certain the shop would be covered, I met with Susan as planned. I put the piece of paper in front of her with the three lines and watched as the slow smile crept across her face. "I love this!"

was her enthusiastic reply. Even though I could tell by her expression long before she spoke the words, I was glad to hear her passionate response.

"I don't have anything else though, Suz. This is it. I thought this was supposed to be so easy, I was so *on* with it all, but I just can't get any more..."

Susan understood my process. Creation was something to be felt, not thought. Multi- sensory experiences also fit in there somewhere, and I always looked for that subtle current. Even when designing pictures with a client, a mat selection was chosen on how I could "taste" the color. I might "feel" sound, but both of these senses transmuted to something vibratory. If it vibrated correctly, I knew it would remain in that form. If not, it would be re-worked. I would not leave it alone until it felt right.

"You'll get it," Susan offered, in her all-knowing, ever-wise and patient teacher's reply. "At some point it will appear. It always does."

"But will it be in time?" I asked. And then the reality hit. We had a production deadline of two months. The songs would have to be crafted <u>and</u> recorded to be placed along with the final edits of the film—this in addition to everything else.

Later that night I turned on the television, trying to distance myself from the temptation of forcing the issue with the song. I watched as the story unfolded to a scene with a character possessed by a strange force of energy. His eyes were whitened by the magic of special effects, suggesting a blindness representing his ability to see things that no one else could.

*And the blindness makes everything clear...*

There it was: the fourth line of the song—but that was all I got. I hastily wrote it down. My gratitude was growing as the words added themselves one to the other, but the smallest part of me recognized the familiar frustration that I would be a slave to this crazy process until it was done.

*As a servant you're more free than ever.*

I let go of the frustration—and thanked my Muse again—only slightly unsettled that the music was revealing itself in an energy unlike anything I had experienced before. What was this? I entered into a new space with this incredible power flowing through me. I only hoped the song could communicate that when it was finished. What if it wasn't "all that and a can of beans," as a friend of mine used to say? My insecurity about being *good enough* rapidly took over and all the what-ifs filled up the space in my mind where the lyrics should be.

They weren't nearly as pleasant a fit. What if my own love of this piece was just me being amazed that I could still write?

*With a mastery over your fear...*came the offering of my Muse.

The song was answering me—and I now felt the vibration that signaled completeness. I reviewed what came together as the lines rearranged themselves in a flow.

*It starts as a drum in the distance,*
*a rhythm of something so strong,*
*And you do what you can to resist this,*
*believing it must be all wrong,*
*'Til the sound fills your head with your heart beat,*

17

*and the blindness makes everything clear*
*As a servant you're more free than ever,*
*with a mastery over your fear.*

I knew I had the first verse. And the power of that "it" — that juice, that spark — that intense pull of energy, had unfolded beautifully for me and was making itself known in this song.

I just didn't know what to call it.

*What was this IT?* I would ask the question in my thoughts, half expecting that the words would tell me themselves as they often did. I sat poised with pen in hand waiting for some sort of movement. Something. Anything. Nothing — again my Muse was on its own time table. So I pleaded: *What do I call you?*

"Nan, honey, the *'it'* is *your* sacred fire." The voice was soft and feminine, not unlike my own, but distinctly different from those times I had spoken out loud.

I looked to see who could possibly be with me in my own computer room. *No one was there.* And while I didn't doubt any of my past experiences with clairvoyance — it actually ran in the family — clairaudience was something *entirely* new. I don't know which was more unnerving: hearing this reassurance spoken by someone who wasn't there, or that she knew my preferred nickname.

As the full realization of what I had experienced washed over me, I gasped with that full hard "breath of life" taken by an emerging human who has been newly birthed. It was as though I had been released from a forced submergence under water, and I could not get enough air...

The chorus of the song was now revealed:

18

*Sacred Fire*
*At the center of the flame*
*Something Higher*
*You know is calling out your name*

My mind began rapid-fire scenes that replayed themselves from my memory banks. For the first time in my life I found myself appreciating my inner geek, left over from high school. Every single reference to sacred fire was called up in panoramic flashes: there was the sacred fire tended by the Vestal Virgins in ancient Rome, believed to be a presence of divinity as long as it was tended. The term of sacred fire was still used by several Native American tribes to reference continuation, and I had an Aboriginal reference too. Something in India? I knew that the Druids — and later their descendants of Celtic clans — had a ritual around it. Why did I want to associate it with Polynesian peoples and Africa?

Part of me wanted to become swept away with the research for what all this meant. It didn't matter. All that was needed was the knowledge that this one reference had shown up on nearly every continent on the globe, through the ages, crossing  timelines and land mass to become a universal representation of humanity's link with divine intelligence. I had succeeded in finding that conceptual framework that I felt would be commonly understood.

My own transformation was beginning also, although it would not become apparent to me for several weeks, and not fully embraced for a couple of years after that.

The deep breath that had filled my lungs following my clairaudient epiphany signaled my defiance to drown, submerged as I was, in the vast ocean of unconsciousness. It planted the seed for a faint but growing understanding —

however abstract—of what I was put on this earth to accomplish.

It would gradually become more apparent after the second verse took form over the next few days:

> *Now understanding your purpose,*
> *the sleeper awakens within*
> *Allowing your greatness to surface,*
> *for the journey that you must begin*
> *For each one of us has been chosen,*
> *to become what we know as Divine*
> *But how many more remain frozen,*
> *waiting until they can find, their*
>
> *Sacred Fire*
> *At the center of the flame*
> *Something higher*
> *You know is calling out your name.*

As much as any art form I had embraced, which at one time had included writing and acting, music had always afforded a tool to inspire, teach, lead, and support others in accepting their own limitations. It provided easy access to inner vision as it offered hope.

And now it had become a vehicle, one which would be transferred in ownership from myself, (the manufacturer) to the listeners (or consumers) so they could then take it for a glorious ride through their own mountains of greatness and valleys of vulnerability. The title that gave proof of that ownership was _feeling_—which would also be the dominant connecting force between true passion and right action, otherwise known as: sacred fire.

All of time slowed in this moment of clarity.

It would still be some time before I learned that my only limitation for "success" was in holding onto the belief that I lacked any power to do this. But in that one moment the dots were starting to connect.

I didn't know how it would all play out exactly. There were some blank spots and a lot of insecurity. Yet I felt certain this would be resolved over time — oddly confident that I could recognize the barriers when they appeared, or be shown by someone else where they were hiding. I would know the right steps to take and feel satisfied that I had everything I needed for the film — as well as the rest of my life.

# Sacred Fire Boarding Pass

PERMISSION · GRANTED · TO · COME · ABOARD

Notes
_____
Journal Entries

# Chapter Three

It's Just Not Right

*"...it's not how fast or far that I go*
*that I came here to learn what I already know,*
*Success is whatever we make it..."*
*...from* Tea with the Girls, *song lyrics*
- Adrianna Larkin -

On this Sunday morning in late August of 2007 I allowed the blue-black funk to keep me company in my favorite easy chair. I ignored the calling from domestic chores, content with Mike's willingness to do dishes. I was taking some time to process the fact that Susan's film would be placed on hold indefinitely for lack of funding. As much as I wanted to see her produce the film, my own agenda was now undeniable.

Susan had given her explanation a couple of days before, all of which made sense, but my disappointment betrayed the amount of emotional equity I had invested in her project. Now I had no choice but to reflect on what this meant for me. *Sacred Fire* replayed over and over in my head in the weeks since I had applied the perfect melody. That had come easily too, weaving its way through the lyrics like an old friend. I could hear the production so clearly with all the instruments.

I was having a hard time accepting that it wouldn't be recorded.

Normally I would analyze a song to death—even after it was done—but this one was different. It was solid. I couldn't wait to hear it with the full instrumentation, and I welcomed the constant replay inside my head. The earwig of my own music usually drove me crazy, but this one just made me more excited. How had I lost that electricity? I was annoyed...and I didn't like having to sort out all of these feelings just because of some stupid song I wrote. How did I get here from there?

I let my mind wander back to the very first time I felt like this. I was 13 years old. My parents, who shared their love of music and theatre, had taken me to a summer stock production of "Fiddler on the Roof." The lead character Tevye was played by Shelley Berman, a Jewish comedian who was often featured on "The Ed Sullivan Show." He frequently did bits flavored with the Yiddish humor that my Dad enjoyed growing up on the East Coast.

On this particular evening I waited patiently for the curtain to rise. As it did, Tevye stood in a spotlight, opening the story with his soliloquy that so beautifully expressed how life is ever changing and precarious...

What happened next was completely unexpected. The costume, the script, and the delivery was so dramatically different than the dry humor I associated with the comedic side of this actor, it was difficult to believe it was the same person! He had been totally transformed by the role...and I was entranced. A growing sense of electricity in my body joined the crescendo of the music and the lights.

And by the time the chorus offered its performance of *Tradition*, I was totally mesmerized and my metamorphosis was complete.

*This is what I want to do*, I thought to myself. *This is it. It all makes sense. I want to make people feel the way I'm feeling now, and I can do this. I already sing, I love costumes, I memorize things easily.* In the mind of a thirteen-year old, it was perfect.

Stage was comfortable—my parents had provided me with one at every opportunity. I would frequently reign as a mini diva, perched on top of my aunt's baby grand where I would perform my little heart out, complete with gestures and facial expressions, joined by a tireless piano player to accompany me, my Aunt Jackie.

I don't ever remember *not* singing. I assumed it had started with visits to my mom's childhood farm in Missouri. Come nightfall everyone took their assigned sleeping spots and I was placed in a trundle bed to keep company with my grandmother. She would share her repertoire of old Irish ballads and delighted in teaching me the words to them all.

By the time I was four, my Dad bought me a little pair of cowboy boots to match those he wore on weekends to that same Missouri farm. Dad was not the one I imitated however. Nancy Sinatra's release, *These Boots Were Made for Walkin'*, was being played on every major radio station in the country. As the natural sponge that four-year-olds tend to be, I soaked up the song. I walked *and* I strutted. Each time the boots went on so did my rendition of Sinatra's hit. In many of the years that followed, I couldn't help but wonder how often Dad regretted making that purchase.

Singing was a constant in my universe; it continued with family functions, chorus in school, and with my favorite albums. But the theatre experience was a turning point after which I landed every part I auditioned for in my high school drama club.

I had found my purpose.

I had always loved playing dress up and let's pretend. In high school I let that little-girl love of imagination welcome the freedom to be somebody other than myself. When I stepped on stage, I wore the life of a character — and I made her real. My own daily reality had me cast in the role of the girl geek. I liked to learn, but the one thing I *hadn't* learned was how to keep quiet about it. Growing up as I had in a suburb of Chicago, surrounded by diversity and a variety of cultures, it didn't seem to be a problem. I could always find someone like me.

But when I was transplanted in the seventh grade to a small rural town, it became a different story. I found myself in a place where the majority of the residents could trace their lineage back three generations or more to their agricultural roots, and they regularly reminded me that I could not. Moreover, my dad was a "Jersey Jew" in a Protestant farming community of less than 2500 people. We were strangers in what seemed — at least to me at the time — like a very strange land.

Being on stage gave some degree of acceptance and periodic relief from the taunts and torment that I had experienced in high school from being a band nerd. When try-outs came, the mockery eased up as I always played a key role in the production of whatever play was being performed at the time.

I usually went for character parts. From *dumb blondes* to *caustic old ladies*, I would take every opportunity to enroll in workshops and audition for community theatre. At 16, I auditioned and received the part of Millie in a local production of the Pulitzer Prize winning play *Picnic*. My joy was short-lived, however, when Mom refused to let me accept the part — the rehearsals would require me to be out too late on a school night.

I applied to drama programs, was accepted by a private college close to home. The big dream was to go to New York, but I already understood that neither funds nor the mindset of my parents would allow for this. By the time I graduated high school, I had memorized complete scores from eight different musicals — all the parts.

I showed the acceptance letter to my Dad when I received it from the college of my choice. I was elated. I couldn't have been more overjoyed if I had received a letter from one of my teen idols. "Are you crazy?" came Dad's less than enthusiastic response. "You'll starve." He already had his mind made up — I was going to the local junior college to get a two-year nursing degree. "Besides, if you still want to do theatre, this won't stop you — and at least you will be able to eat…" It was logical. I was practical — or at least I chose to be in order to end the conflict.

I completed a nursing program in two years, accelerating beyond the norm of three years that most people took to get through it. It was just far enough away from home and had no dormitory, so my parents helped me find a small apartment. By the end of my first year I had gone through all the money I saved and the student loan taken on to offset this expense.

Opting again for practicality — and necessity — I took a job working nights as an aide. My hours were increased to full time as I completed my second year of school. I was exhausted. Working full time and going to school full time for something that seemed only a means to an end was breaking my spirit. Adding to this was an unknown predisposition to anemia that was being tilted by lack of sleep, poor diet, and the duress of nursing school.

I continued on nights for a while after graduation, and the anemia was discovered when I almost passed out on my shift. Sleep deprivation was not a valid enough argument for the hospital administration to take me off nights, so I changed jobs and moved to evenings. Life got a little better with the elevation of red blood cells and a job that meshed with my internal body clock.

All remnants of a career that had anything to do with music or theatre was carefully packed away as I focused on my marriage and a new position in the emergency room. I was already in my mid-twenties and completely swept up in this field of nursing that was so new to me. I flourished in the fast-paced demands of an environment where I had to draw on my intellect to shift gears rapidly. By the time my son was born at age 28, all attention was focused on work, motherhood, and a marriage that had begun to circle the drain.

Emergency room staff had one of the highest ratios for divorce of any department in the hospital, much of it being attributed to the amount of stress and the reality of life that one can never avoid. One co-worker offered his perspective. "I have no tolerance for an argument about taking out the trash when I lost a four-year-old who died on my shift."

I had joined that group of statistics with my first marriage, but weighed it heavily against the possibilities for success as I entered into a second union. I left the ER to join husband number two, a piano tuner, in his business. I was 34 years old. It seemed like a good match initially as we were both musicians. I had returned to playing guitar and had started crafting songs, but as time progressed it became apparent that we were better able to fine tune our respective instruments than we were a successful partnership. As that marriage disintegrated, I found myself back in the job market again.

Between the two marriages I had completed my bachelor's degree in nursing. This gave me a few more options for re-entry into a gainfully employed state. I landed comfortably and gratefully in corporate America and discovered that I could transfer my skills of triage in the emergency room to the priorities of the corporate "life blood." Within two years I was promoted to the management level.

All the while crafting songs.

When my first marriage ended, I had looked to music to offset the human drama that followed me home every night from the ER...used it as a place to hide, or at least distance myself from everything I needed to forget about the day. I had played flute in high school, but neither this nor the piano was quiet enough to let a baby sleep in the other room. So I wrote music as a way of teaching myself to play guitar. It cost nothing and, moreover, it allowed a 14-month old to remain undisturbed.

My influences were the folk divas of the 70s: Carol King, Carly Simon, Joan Baez, and Judy Collins. I had a special focus on story-telling. The imagery afforded by word painters like Gordon Lightfoot and Billy Joel set the bar for the power communicated with the lyrics of a song.

My son David was the inspiration for much of my music. I crafted a lullaby, appropriately titled "David's Song", and expressed my wide range of emotions around motherhood, including the unique aspect of doing it single handedly in "The Only One." I experimented with blues and fell in love with Latin rhythms. The only thing that I felt limited by was my ability to play guitar. I was too busy writing music to learn the nuances of the instrument.

As I began to see my *hobby* and the songs it produced taking shape, it made sense to apply what I knew about marketing, budgets, customer service—all elements that I instantly understood in the business world—to the *business* of music. If I could package my product to engage the market, I might just be able to get that coveted commercial release. If the right artist added it to their album, who knows where it would go?

"Whether you are billing yourself as a singer or not, you are expected to have a CD in the music industry—it's your calling card," I was advised by one producer.

So I made my first CD as a marketing piece, my calling card. And I took it traveling. Upon my first major songwriting seminar in Nashville I exchanged a brief conversation with a representative from Sony music who seemed completely taken by the first track "Sister Mississippi." He held it up in the workshop as a paragon of the perfect folk song. "It tells a story...this is what a great song does."

I approached him later to ask, "If you really liked it, where do we go from here?"

"Absolutely nowhere—it is a great song, I love it, it's just not commercial...there's a difference."

The second CD—"Coming Home"—was crafted in response to feedback I was receiving to keep the songs sparse without much instrumentation. The elements of composition needed to be heard. This standard had already been reversed by the time the CD was pressed. In spite of that, a publishing house had taken an interest in one song entitled "Perception" offering to do a little research and to see if it could be pitched to the Dixie Chicks to record.

But the fates, timing—or maybe my recalcitrant Muse had other things in mind. That meeting occurred just days before the Dixie Chicks had received national exposure and a wealth of criticism for what many deemed unpopular political views—after which time the publisher quit returning my calls.

Then there was the A&R (artist and repertoire) guy from Virgin Records Nashville, with whom I had developed a working relationship to get feedback on what he was seeking for emerging artists. He liked my music and we hit it off, but I knew him all of about three weeks before that division of Virgin records was reportedly taken over by Capitol and all staff were released to cleanse the old regime. No information was available regarding his whereabouts.

I was collecting as many "almost" scenarios as I was rejection letters. The letter collection had grown larger too. I believed I had enough paper to do a wall, and I saved each and every one of them with the warped intent of doing exactly that one day. Some of them were caustic, others were kind.

Many were inconsistent, frequently bordering on the humorous. I would send a song which generated a response that the production was weak, but they had unlimited praise for the talent picked to do the vocals. The next response might advise that I have someone do the song who could *really* sing because the vocalist was taking away from an otherwise solid production. In all cases, the vocalist—and producer—was *me*.

The funniest of them all was when I received two very oppositional responses similar to those above, following the review of the same song by two different people *at the same company*!

That I could call all of this up with such clarity told me how weird this business was and how stacked against me it all seemed. And now...*Sacred Fire* would not even be recorded? What was wrong with all of this? What was wrong with *me*?

I extracted myself from my easy chair that had become comfortably cushioned with self pity to pull down the very first CD, "No Ingénue," for a nostalgic listen. I had to know if I had any talent at all or if I was just kidding myself.

I recalled what it felt like to go into that huge commercial studio for the first time and watch the session players light up with each new song. They and the engineer often commented on what they liked about a certain chord progression, tempo or lyric thread. It was a blast to work with them. As I listened to the first three tracks, I was surprised to realize how good the songs sounded to me even a decade later. I especially noticed how much of that synergy could still be heard.

I called to my husband Mike who was in the kitchen, "You know, before I die, one of the things I would *love* to do as part of my bucket list is to cut another album with these guys—it was so much fun." Mike barely paused before he came out drying his hands on a dish towel. "Then why don't you?" he asked.

"You're kidding. We don't have the money for that right now. Everything is going back into the gallery." My pragmatic side was defending its turf.

"If you want to do it, let's find a way. Why don't you start by making some calls to see if you can even get in touch with those guys. That's the first step. See if they're even still in the area—how long has it been?"

32

My heart sank. "Ten years for Benet, the drummer — and a few years for Dave and Tom. I don't even know where Jack the engineer is. He was part of that whole energy too. Even if I found numbers, I'm not certain they would be available or would want to..."

Mike's eagerness for me to return to what I loved could not be contained. I could see it on his face. We had been together seven years already and had become completely transparent to one another. He had learned from past experience that he could not argue a hard stance with me in this state of self doubt. Instead he chose the perfect position of gentle coaxing. "Why don't you *try?*" he said shrugging his shoulders, "You can always decide where to go from there."

A little research online and contacts through other musicians put me in touch with everyone I wanted to reach.

Late in October of 2007, when the project was supposed to be completed to be added to the Susan's full length feature, it was just beginning. The crew, Dave Black on lead guitar, Tom Maloney on bass, and Benet Schaeffer on drums had all resumed the roles they had played in my first project, once again under the engineering direction of Jack Petracek. I had found them all — and now I was recording my fourth CD. This collective of musicians was phenomenal — the artists touted as some of the best players in St. Louis — which is why they had been chosen by the studio as session players ten years ago.

Now I was the one contacting them directly and they were not only available but each expressed an eagerness to do another project of my original music. Chris Voelker was added — I knew him to be an extremely gifted violin player whom I had hired many times for the shop to provide music during our art events. Sandy Weltman provided amazing harmonica tracks. With the reputations of these later additions that placed them in that "best player" category as well, it turned out to be an all star cast. It was more than I could have asked for, but it was only the icing on the cake.

As an added bonus, engineer Jack would record many of the tracks in his home studio, a benefit we didn't have ten years earlier when the technology was so new. Having a high-quality home studio made the project much more cost effective.

Additionally I had picked up a well-paying gig averaging twice a month on weekend evenings when the shop closed. This allowed for the recording fees to be paid as we went along. One year after we began the process, the CD was complete. On October 16, 2008 I performed with four of the five musicians on the album at the CD release party.

It was my first time ever performing live with more than two musicians, let alone this amazing group of players. Not only had they made themselves available for the music, but also for this celebration of yet another return to my craft.

It was made even more special for me in that my son ran sound for the event. From the corner of my sight I could see him occasionally lost in thought and shaking his head.

"Problems?" I asked after it was over.

"Nothing that I didn't expect—there were some limitations with the equipment, the glass of the atrium-type room called for some adjustments...all stuff that comes with running sound." My son, now 22, had far surpassed anything I could do on guitar or a sound board.

"I was worried when I saw you shaking your head," I confessed.

"Oh...that," he laughed. "I just couldn't decide if I should laugh hysterically or curse the unfairness of it all. Watching you guys up there completely floored me. I have to tell you Mom, as a musician myself I couldn't help but be a bit jealous."

"Jealous?"

"Well, yeah. I knew it had been nearly two months since all of you were even in the same room together, and you just walked up there with no rehearsal and pulled out this great performance—like you all do this every night. It's obvious the guys really dig the stuff you write…and their skill is amazing, but from where I sat—even knowing you were nervous—it was like the music was *creating itself*."

He returned to shaking his head with what was now fully evident as disbelief—all the while laughing—as he added: "It's just not right."

# Sacred Fire Boarding Pass

PERMISSION · GRANTED · TO · COME · ABOARD

Notes
___

Journal Entries

# Chapter Four

·﹀﹀﹀·

## I Know This Guy — His Name is Mike

*"'I'm Missouri born and bred' she said*
*as he tipped his hat she shook her head,*
*didn't really matter what he said, he would have to show her."*
*...from* Missouri Born, *song lyrics*
*- Adrianna Larkin -*

Weeks later I would still reflect on the irony that was so evidently apparent in the conversation with my son. I became clearly aware of how close I had come to sabotaging it all. My husband Mike had been the catalyst for moving it forward, holding my vision when I could no longer hold it for myself. With every turn he was there to help problem solve and encourage me. I realized, in a mental repeat performance, that my most prized asset was a partner who was both my best friend and biggest fan — but I had almost sabotaged that encounter too.

The unlikely courtship between Mike and I began with a blind date arranged by people we both worked with. Well, not exactly blind, maybe...

Just visually impaired.

A co-worker at the insurance company where I was employed was dating a man who worked at a pharmaceutical plant. Her boyfriend worked with this guy...he was recently divorced. She'd met him...he was really nice...his name was Mike...and I listened to the familiar buildup waiting for the ultimate question: Would I go out with him?

*Oh well. What's one more duck in the shooting gallery of my love life*, I thought.

I had been doing some dating online, but having left a serious relationship less than six months earlier I wasn't eager to get all that serious again. I had also become fairly jaded. The *yes* I gave my co-worker in an effort to end the conversation and get back to what I was doing, jumped miles ahead of the thought stream that soon followed.

I was preparing to cross over to the land where I promised I would never go: the land of the newly-divorced and walking wounded. I imagined a dinner date where the conversation revolved around a whiny account of how much he missed his wife...or worse yet, how his broken heart would never allow him to trust again...

Well, maybe he wouldn't call.

Two days later my phone rang. It was Mike the Guy, and he seemed pretty upbeat. Upbeat enough to catch me off guard and offer to meet for coffee. He had seen my picture online through my music website, but I had no idea what he looked like.

"How will I know you?" I asked.

"Well, I have brown hair, a bit of a receding hairline…carrying a few extra pounds—I wear glasses."

*My God*, I thought, *HE'S A TROLL.* In my cynical and much-jaded mind I had formulated the belief that ALL men ALWAYS exaggerate their good looks. If he was freely mentioning attributes that would keep him off the cover of *Gentleman's Quarterly*, what did he REALLY look like? I let my mind race, as I imagined something akin to Jabba the Hutt from the *Star Wars* trilogy, with an odd fringe of hair joining his two ears that supported cinder-block glasses.

Looks had not been a deal breaker for me in the past—quite the opposite in fact. I always sought the cerebral connection. The last relationship that had lasted over 4 years was with a man 12 years my senior who was not quite five foot tall. I on the other hand was 5 foot 7. But I was not getting a mind connection with the guy over the phone. He was nice, but not captivating. Well, it was only coffee.

We agreed to meet at a local bookstore with a café, and upon my arrival it was almost empty. There was only one other guy, lean and well muscled—he was looking down at his pager that had just gone off. We passed each other and shared the polite but slightly awkward smile that gets exchanged when two strangers accidentally make eye contact. He had glasses, but nothing I could detect as a receding hairline. He also looked to be in great shape. *Nope,* I thought, *not a troll — it can't be him.*

Soon the one lone man made his way back from the pay phone. Extending his hand he smiled and said, "Hi, I'm Mike…sorry I walked past you when you first came in. My daughter just paged me and she's 13 and home alone. I wanted to make sure she was OK."

A cup of coffee for each of us and a cookie that I would purchase made up the meal for that meeting. Noncommittal pleasantries were exchanged. I noticed his hands were shaking. He noticed me noticing—and offered an explanation: "This is a little new for me. I was married 18 years..."

*Here it comes,* I thought, waiting for the whiny account of his story to unfold.

"I'm not used to dating—guess I'm a little nervous." The admission was accompanied by a shy and slightly boyish smile, and perfectly punctuated by the spilling of his coffee. Both of us grabbed for the extra napkins and tried to undo the worst of the damage. As we grabbed plates and cups, blotting up the soggy mess, I realized that the cookie which was to be my lunch had instead been converted to a pile of crumbs that I nervously made into my own little tabletop sandbox. It was becoming evident that Mike the Guy wasn't the only one who felt out of place.

Mike later revealed that he left my company to join his friend at a bar that evening. "She's not going out with me again," he had confided to his buddy, "I just know it."

Valentine's Day was four days later and my online acquaintances let it pass without an e-card, gag gift or even an honorable mention. But that was what I had asked for, nothing serious. Still, it would be nice to not feel isolated.

And just as I had decided that Valentine's Day was my most hated not-even-really-a-holiday holiday, Mike the Guy e-mailed me: "Happy Valentines Day. I hope you are having a great time." It was simple. It was thoughtful— considerate, not pushy...*OK, what's his angle?* My cynicism tried to cover the fact that I was both intrigued and touched.

A follow-up phone call to thank him seemed in order. Somewhere in the conversation I revealed I was performing at a coffee house near my home on Saturday.

"I would really like to hear you," he eagerly chimed in. "What time do you play?"

"Ten a.m. I just do a couple of hours." As I gave him the location and he calculated that it was close to a 45-minute drive from his house, his tone of voice shifted to what seemed like genuine disappointment. "I'm working nights on Friday, so I'll have to see how I feel when I get off that morning."

*He's not coming,* I thought to myself. *It's too much trouble. Anytime a guy has to travel or be inconvenienced in any way, it ain't gonna happen...*

Saturday morning I arrived at the coffee shop shortly before 9:40, managing my sound equipment with the process I had efficiently designed. The amp that I used for my performance to balance the vocals and guitar weighed about 40 pounds, but would stack on a dolly with a duffle bag of cords on top. The case of CDs available for sale would rest on top of this. The microphone stand would be balanced precariously on one corner—and all of this could be managed by one hand while my other hand carried the guitar. I would stand the guitar upright and balance it against my hip as my elbow supported the top of the case freeing a hand to grab the door handle which would then be held open by my foot until I could get a shoulder in.

In this pose that made me look more like a Dr. Seuss illustration than a skilled performer, I would occasionally capture the attention of a kind soul who would offer assistance. On this day a friendly male hand had reached over my shoulder to grab the door and relieve me of the juggling act I performed as I stood on one foot. The one benefit of taking martial arts all those years was that I had developed a good sense of balance. I hung there a minute before I looked up to offer a smile and a nod of thanks to my unknown benefactor.

It took a moment to process the familiarity, but I knew this guy. It was Mike.

"This is for you." I looked down at the purple rose he held in his other hand. Then I handed him the guitar and took the rose. It was only later I would process how much trust was already innately there—I don't hand my guitar to just anyone.

"I guess you didn't have to work last night," I found myself saying.

"No, I had to work, I just got off. I showered and came over. I haven't been to bed yet."

"You're kidding. I thought *I* was short on sleep. I didn't get to bed until almost 4:00 this morning because I went to Nashville and back for a pitch session."

He looked wistful, pausing just a moment before he said, "I would have gone with you." It took a much shorter moment for him to realize that he'd actually spoken the thought out loud, and the up-tempo backpedaling began.

"I mean...you could have slept with me if we drove together."

This wasn't getting any better. The color had drained from his face with that last statement as he realized what actually came out of his mouth. It was becoming painful to watch.

"I didn't mean sleep *with* me...I meant..." Oh man, he was sinking fast. I had to throw the boy a rope.

"I know what you meant, it's OK," I laughed. I thought it was kind of cute. He was really trying to be polite, but just getting off the graveyard shift his mouth was a few steps ahead of his brain. I knew all too well the telltale signs of the night-worker-wind-down. It was almost 10 a.m. *He should be going to bed now,* I thought. *But he came to see me.*

He stayed for the entire performance—and before leaving he asked if I'd like to see a movie with him that night.

"Only if we can get a nap first—but not together," I said, making light of our earlier conversation.

I laughed.

He blushed.

Later that night I was not prepared for what would take place in the theatre. Agreeing to my choice of a romantic comedy, I knew that my brand of humor would be a new experience for him. I seldom even chuckle at the obvious sight gags, but can rouse a good belly laugh with subtext. This usually means I am the only one laughing at parts just a few people get, and I'm quiet when the rest of the theater is roaring with slapstick humor. But on this night we were laughing in unison. My bizarre and frequently irreverent humor had company...and it was good to be understood.

He seemed to *get* me, and I felt like I was starting to know him—this guy named Mike.

And he would prove to me later how often he knew me better than myself.

After four months of steady courtship we had already established what we desired in a partner, noting the surprising compatibility in those desires. We had managed to talk *about* marriage without ever talking about *our* marriage. I made it abundantly clear to Mike the Guy that I held very few illusions about the trappings of matrimony.

"You know, in the past I have made a big deal about the ring and all that jazz, but for the right person, I would get married with a cigar band," I stated.

He laughed and offered, "Well, I can see where a girl would like a really nice ring. And if the guy really loves her, he doesn't mind getting her something she can show off to her friends."

I had shared my opinion that the money spent on a wedding was inversely proportional to the success of a marriage, and he offered that he thought small ceremonies were more meaningful, but it was cool to have a huge gathering of friends to celebrate — even if it was a reception in the backyard.

On a long weekend trip we stopped at a motel to spend the night. As we were unpacking, Mike produced a small green velvet box from his overnight case — the perfect size and shape for a ring — and casually handed it to me saying, "Here, this is for you."

My acceptance was not unlike that of someone being gifted the carcass of a dead rodent. I cautiously grasped the box with two fingers as something that I really did not wish to make contact with any more than necessary. *What was he thinking?* Yep, it was a ring box. I had made the determination after examining it from all sides in my reluctance to confirm its contents. *He couldn't be serious.* We had barely been dating four months! It was too soon…too soon…too soon. I could feel the panic rising in me like a tsunami. *How was I going to get out of this?* I didn't want to hurt his feelings. I *really* liked him, I believed I *loved* him, but marriage? *NOW?*

"Open it," he said. The degree of pleasure he had with himself in presenting this to me was now evident in his face. This was going to be even worse that I thought.

"I don't…know…" my voice trailed off, but his smile remained.

"Just open it." He seemed so certain. *He obviously has no idea how I feel,* I thought to myself.

I gulped hard and opened the small velvet box with

all of the climactic suspense surrounding the next victim of a horror film—I think I actually expected something to jump out and bite me.

What I saw made me pause, and stare with a mix of disbelief and joy as I held my sides and laughed out loud. The open box wobbled on my hand, then began to blur as tears streamed down my face.

But I never lost my focus on the center of the box that held a perfectly placed cigar band.

He put his arms around me. "Now I thought you might think it was too soon, but I am offering this up as a sort of 'promise ring'—and when you're ready, we can go shopping for the real thing."

In the days and months and years that followed, Mike the Guy demonstrated many times that he knew me pretty well after all, but it was never more evident than those times when I wanted to give it all up.

His innate knowledge and sensitivity, combined with his ability to do damage control for the worst of my self-destructive tendencies, was a saving grace that I could not ignore. In a pivotal moment that seemed to obliterate any connection with a destiny linked to music, his emotional intelligence spoke the prophecy of its return.

It had occurred on one of the many trips to Nashville—our last in fact before purchasing the shop. The argument seemed to go on forever, but in reality was quite brief. We had come away from our last meeting, following a whirlwind of appointments with publishers and artist representatives, trying to get them to pick up just one song for a commercial release. Upon return to the motel room, I erupted in a volcano of molten emotion.

"I can't do this anymore," I said. "I'm done."

My voice was rapidly nearing the pitch that could

45

only be heard by members of the canine family, but my husband was the voice of assurance.

"We can do this, babe, another 5 years...I'm sure in that time—"

"You don't understand," I cut him off, "I've been pitching songs for fifteen years already. Fifteen years..."

"You didn't have me then," he grinned. He was so confident. I was so tired.

"No, I can't," I replied.

"Two years then, honey, just give me two years..." The bartering had begun. "I really think..."

But I cut him short again. "I can't." My voice had changed to almost a whine. "Look, I'm tired, I'm finished—I tried, but I just don't have what it takes. I get that, so that's it. It was a good run, but I don't want to do music anymore."

He paused for a moment to let me run out of steam. I had reached a new level of insistence, and I was convinced he did not know who he was dealing with. I thought to myself, *he can't possibly understand. You can only be told so many times that you're not good enough.*

Mike had been by my side and on call for the whole music scene since we were married. I had coached him in the industry lingo. His gentle persuasion and persistence, along with the willingness to don cowboy boots on a moment's notice, had opened the doors that I had been knocking on for more than a decade. We could get the meetings, just not the deal.

"Take a break then," he said.

"NO...you don't get it. I'm finished, done...I QUIT!"

He waited a moment before speaking. His arms came around me and he offered the soft voice of unconditional love. "You need a break," he said. "You're tired and I get that, but you're not going to quit—you can't." He kissed my temple then quietly said:

"This is who you are."

# Sacred Fire Boarding Pass

PERMISSION·GRANTED·TO·COME·ABOARD

Notes
___
Journal Entries

# Chapter Five

## Skin Tight

*"I know you could read my face, I didn't want to reveal my hand,*
*But I need you to understand about a seed planted a long time ago*
*that waits for Spring to bloom."*
*...from* Warm Spring Rain, *song lyrics*
*- Adrianna Larkin -*

Mike had been right all along, of course, although I wouldn't start to admit it until the emergence of *Sacred Fire*. Even though I protested that there was not time for writing, performance, *and* the demands of the shop, I didn't quit— not even with raging self doubt and a business to run. I would find some excuse or opportunity that would place me on stage at least a handful of times in the history of the gallery. One such situation occurred on a Saturday evening after closing, when Mike and I went out to dinner, mainly to take in the entertainment.

The singer booked that night was a name very well known to me as well as to millions of others. Mae Wheeler, jazz legend and St. Louis icon, was more than just friend or mentor. She was like family. Mae had offered me my first spot in a high profile venue performing in her "Diva '98" production, featuring the best of female voices in St. Louis. It was because of her I had stood on the same stage where I had watched B.B. King perform just a few years earlier.

We arrived at the end her first set, just in time to make a place for her at our table where she joined us on her break.

"Start warmin' up Baby, you're covering my break," she said.

"I don't think so, Mae...I'm retired."

"Honey, I'm 71 years old. I'm not *ever* gonna retire, and I'm not going to let *you* retire either. It's too much in your blood."

This was beginning to sound familiar. On this night, it was becoming evident I was outclassed and outgunned. Mike had sided with Mae against me.

"You heard the lady," he grinned as he continued. "Get up there." He was quite pleased with himself. The waiter placed a meal in front of Mae and flashed a smile that matched the other two at the table. It was enough to make me wonder if he was in on this too. If so, it made for a tight-knit little conspiracy.

"Mae, I can't," I said.

But she persisted. "Well, somebody's got to entertain these people, and I have to eat, so get up there."

I politely declined. Then I said no. I offered my reasons. I declined again.

Then I sang.

I loved Mae, I adored my husband. I would not be shamed by anything, but love was a force too great to fight and there was an intensity building around all of this. I also knew that some part of me could not live with myself if I didn't do this. After it was all over, I felt a very slight return of that electricity. It was barely enough to register—and it was tempered with a certain degree of relief—but it was there.

Mae was relentless in making her point that I could not be allowed to retire. I would find myself as a featured performer in a number of Mae Wheeler productions, one of which overlapped with the recording I was doing for the *Sacred Fire* album. This one was to take place at The Sheldon Concert Hall.

The black formal I had selected for that evening's performance had groupings of spaghetti straps whose complex design would permit entry only with a Rosetta stone *and* a secret password. I had waited until the last minute to get dressed as I tried to quell my mounting anxiety. Now, I had to rush.

Mike was already dressed for the evening and ready to go when he walked in on me wrestling with my gown. He later agreed with my analogy that in that light, poised as I was, with only hands emerging from the top of the dress—tangled in the spaghetti straps and waving wildly—I resembled a large fabric celery stick.

"I can't..." I was fighting the urge to hyperventilate. "I can't...get...into...this...dress!" I was losing the battle to panic. I questioned why I had agreed to do this. I questioned everything. If this was supposed to be in my blood, wasn't I supposed to at least be comfortable with it?

"Here," came the patient voice I knew so well. "Let me help." Mike untangled my hands and placed them through the arms of the sleeves. Using the same voice that one would use to calm a two-year old into his pajamas, he offered his comic relief. "You know, babe, I think we have this backwards. I'm supposed to help get you *out* of your clothes, not into them."

The humor would be lost on me until later. There were still the shoes to contend with. The ankle strapped satin pumps I had purchased matched the dress so beautifully. And they would have worked great—if the dress hadn't held a grudge.

The shoes had the tiniest of buckles that required microscopic vision in order to fasten them, and the dress had no intention of allowing that proximity. The fabric would not yield its restraint enough for me to bend and reach the tiny buckle, nor would it allow me to bend my leg behind me to reach it that way either. Mike knelt down to complete this last detail for me.

We arrived at the Sheldon where the performance was scheduled and I stared at the building before going in. I had a history with this place. That—I decided—was the real source of my angst.

I found myself transported in my thoughts to my second CD release on a January evening six years ago. It had been scheduled at "The acoustically perfect Sheldon Concert Hall" on Washington Avenue in St. Louis. A flood of memories returned as I called up the predicted ice storm, the ticket outlet misreporting that my show was cancelled, and a series of other events that limited the attendance of my debut at this major venue. Limited was an understatement.

In an auditorium that seated 720 people, I had an audience of eight.

Eight.

I became lost in my thoughts as I recalled how I had finished the first hour of that concert and looked out among the faces. I had conferred with the two players featured on this second CD—Dave Black and Sandy Weltman—who had made themselves available to be with me this night. We talked about calling the show done after the first hour. Something inside of me vetoed that decision. It's not that I loved the stage. Performance of my own music was something that never came as easily as writing or recording it. And it wasn't like the eight people in the audience would have rushed the stage and taken me down out of protest. These were my closest friends and they would have completely understood.

But in my mind, eight people had paid to see a two-hour program and eight people deserved a show. I excused myself from the green room and my two companion performers to be alone for a few minutes.

"I don't get it." I was having my own conversation with God and frankly, I was pissed.

"Eight people—seriously, EIGHT—are you kidding me?" The tears were welling up and I knew I couldn't contain them much longer. "I'm supposed to do *this*? Be tortured and tormented? *This* is who I am, a musical artist who can't get more than eight f'n people to show up for her CD release? Well, YOU of all people know how stubborn I can be and YOU of all people will know that I speak from my heart when I say this…"

I was now continuing between sobs. "I *will* finish this concert. I *will* give eight people a show they will remember and feel good about paying for, but when it's done, *SO AM I*. You are going to have to give me one HELL of a sign to ever, EVER open that guitar case again…and you know I MEAN IT!"

I composed myself, re-applied my make-up, returned on stage and noticed immediately that something had changed. My eyes scanned the audience as they had during my opening song when I had recognized one person who,

53

surprisingly enough, was not related to me in any way. Let's call her lucky number eight.

I hadn't really expected God to be listening — certainly hadn't expected such an immediate response when he had so many crucial things to be tending to. But I was no longer performing to an audience of eight. I counted again, just to be certain: one, two, three, four, five, six, seven....

Yep, lucky number eight had left at intermission.

Still, the show went on. Halfway through the second set, I noticed a lanky male figure dancing in front of the stage. I heard some murmurings and watched as this new "number eight" moved wildly around the periphery of the performance area becoming more animated with each song.

Finally, the last song was sung — with no one in my collection of family or friends having any idea of the bargain I had made. I paused a moment to look at my guitar. I would miss it, but it would be OK.

Two of my closest friends descended on me almost out of breath after the performance. "Beatle Bob is here," they offered in unison.

"Who...what?" I was trying to process what I should know about this.

My friend Barb repeated the statement with the same breathless wonder: "Beatle Bob is here...it's a *sign*."

"Yes, yes..." the remaining voices gathered around me and chimed in: "It's a sign."

Beatle Bob was a bit of color and whimsy that was seldom appreciated in St. Louis at that time, although he was increasingly being called upon to emcee music festivals across the country. He would later gain national recognition as sort of a media personality and there would be a documentary made about his life. Beatle Bob was reported to have attended at least one concert a night since 1996. The musical myth tied to the legend of the man was that his appearance served as a sign of destined success for whatever group of performers graced the stage that night, as he was extremely music savvy and only drawn to the best of the best. I could not contain my curiosity:

"So, what brought you here tonight?" I asked.

He replied, "I was surprised I had never heard of you before…but I had to see for myself the quality act that could have two of the finest players in St. Louis to back *her* up." He then went on to indicate that he was not disappointed.

A few years later Beatle Bob would be a guest on my radio program. In the course of the interview I took the opportunity to publicly share my gratitude for his timely appearance, and he responded that he remembered that evening very well — as well as the circumstances of weather and other events that created the limited attendance.

"I *do* remember that performance…you three performed like you were performing in front of 800 people instead of eight…" He went on to say that there was no decline in the degree of enthusiasm and creativity he witnessed that night, adding: "I applaud all three of you…"

I snapped back to the present moment. Remembering the history of this building that I was preparing to enter for yet another performance made me aware of an emerging pattern: Defeat, surrender, return…defeat, surrender, return. Not unlike the shampoo bottle that instructed me to lather, rinse, repeat…

So here I was, in my brilliantly untangled black dress, walking into the place where, once again, I had almost thrown in the towel: *The acoustically perfect Sheldon Concert Hall on Washington Avenue in St. Louis.* This event was already showing signs of being quite different in that it was very well attended. Mae's productions usually were. Yet, I was feeling no more at peace than the night when I performed to a scant crowd of eight people.

I realized at that moment that I had blamed many things for my discomfort — from clothes to The Creator — but the true source of my distress went much deeper.

I had yet to learn how to be comfortable in my own skin.

# Chapter Six

## Drama and Dramamine

*"The source of all knowledge would tell us*
*to open our hearts that we may hear,*
*if we channel love around us in a prism*
*we would not be a prisoner to our fear."*
*...from* Full Circle, *song lyrics*
*- Adrianna Larkin -*

Standing in the Green Room at the Sheldon, I couldn't help but wonder: what was this strange love/hate relationship that I had with my craft? I loved songwriting. Returning to the studio to record another album was wonderful. But something about being on stage singing my own stuff, no matter how it came off, always left me feeling inadequate.

I had done corporate training and public speaking and actually enjoyed it. I had any number of stages as a kid, and later in high school. Why would this or any other venue make me such a wreck? I had to wonder what part of my "destiny" was served by constantly second guessing myself. If I couldn't be comfortable, I could only hope that this insecurity served some sort of purpose.

Many performers talk about having that "edge" that hones their focus at the beginning of the performance. They describe it as a kind of low level apprehension that takes place at the start of the show but starts to fade when they find their groove. I never got that. Saying "yes" always seemed like a good idea when I was offered a gig; but somewhere between heading for the location and the time I walked off stage at the end of a performance, it became evident I had taken complete leave of my senses.

I was now coming to terms with the fact that this night was not going to be any different. I would have to do what I always did: "fake it" by acting like a singer.

Acting had become my saving grace. In fact, I would focus more on performing a role as a class act than I would the delivery of the song. After all, playing the part of someone else was something I was good at. As musician turned mainstream in the business world, I often left the quirky and creative part of myself behind to *act* like someone groomed for corporate America. Ironically, it was now my business brain that was telling me it was time to act like a first-rate performer.

So on this night I would once again do what I had done so many other times in the past—I would find my center, fill the space of the role, and offer everything I had to command the attention of that room, putting on the best show possible. If a mistake was made, or any weakness felt, I would just keep going. The trick—as someone once said—was never saying "oops" when you forgot your lines. It was the only way I knew to transmute the overwhelming presence of nausea and nerves to something that was functional.

Tom Maloney and Dave Black, who were actively working on the *Sacred Fire* project, had agreed to meet me at

The Sheldon to round out the music. It was January 2008 and we were 3 months into the *Sacred Fire* CD. They knew the material and understood my desire to be free from the guitar on this one night so I could fully animate the performance.

Both had earlier engagements that would put them at the venue extremely close to show time, but at least they were available. Their presence alone was a relief. I knew they had intricate knowledge of the Sheldon's acoustics having both performed there before.

Built at the turn of the 20th century as an opera house in the days before amplification, The Sheldon was proudly described as being "acoustically perfect." It had been designed in such a way that from any seat in the house you could easily hear the presentation from the stage... translation being that any amplification had to be handled with a precise amount of care, so as not to overpower and take away from the performance.

The stage manager arrived to say I had not done my sound check and we were getting ready to start.

"I'm waiting on my band," I said. The panic he was struggling to suppress was clearly evident in his face.

"OK, do you know when they're going to arrive?"

"Put me at the bottom of the line-up," I said. "I'm sure they will get here by then."

"So, who's with you?" he asked.

"Dave Black and Tom Maloney — Dave's on lead and Tom's on bass." I saw the relief wash over his face and he smiled. "Cool. I don't have to worry about those guys — we're fine." His reassuring smile and pat on the shoulder were welcomed gifts.

I breathed a sigh of relief when Tom called to say that he was in the area, but looking for a place to park as the rather small parking lot at The Sheldon was already filled.

Dave had arrived a bit earlier and was waiting along with the other performers. I went to thank him for what I imagined to be the 14th time and to let him know Tom was on his way.

"I'm really glad you're here," I told him. "I have to admit that even after all this time I still get pretty uptight with these things." I promised myself that this would be my last confession before putting on my game face, as I offered a silent blessing for his being there.

He looked thoughtful — and was quiet for one of those seconds-seem-like-hours kind of moments. "I think it must be hard to do your own stuff," he said, "much more than cover tunes. Your heart and soul are 'out there' for the entire world to see. That makes you vulnerable...it would be difficult for anyone." And I blessed him again for giving definition to something I'd yet been able to completely understand.

The first number was done and we waited to rotate out for the second. Upon entering the stage for the second time, we were met with resounding applause. It became more distant, however, as I took my cue and focused on assuming my role.

When the song was over we returned to the Green Room to wait for the grand finale, when all performers would be out on stage together.

"Now I want you to notice something," Tom began. Always the consummate teacher, he usually had something to offer for the benefit of any talent around him. "They weren't applauding for *me* — and they weren't applauding for Dave. When we walked out there, they were applauding for YOU. Did you hear that?"

"Yeah, I know," I said, thinking the point was made and he would be done with it, and feeling a little uncomfortable with such a compliment in the company of these two guys.

"And I just want you to know, I'm not doing this again." He paused to smile as he addressed both me and Mike who was now at my side, "UNLESS, you promise to apply for Austin City Limits—because I'm telling you Nan, you and your music are every bit as good as anyone I have seen showcased there. Do you understand?"

"OK, OK," I said, trying to remain in diva mode. The truth was, I was having a hard time taking him seriously, and he knew it.

Although I had minimized the conversations with both musicians, I appreciated their support and vote of confidence. Any time to reflect on what was shared or their degree of sincerity was short-lived, however, as my exit from The Sheldon that night immediately returned me to my other role: that of the over-burdened business owner.

Largely due to fluctuating gas prices and the residential increase in utility bills, we experienced the worst loss on record in October 2007, just two weeks after starting to record *Sacred Fire*. Since then it had been a roller coaster ride of extremes that caused us to focus more on damage control than on growth.

Mike and I shared our moments together taking stock and even examining options available to us now that all children were out of the house. Selling our home was quickly ruled out, as we had refinanced the house to fund the growth of our business in the first two years. The burst of the housing market bubble and declining values had caused our home to be worth much less than what we owed on it.

Our 401ks and savings had been wiped out long ago in the purchase and early growth stages of our business.

We considered other options which included one of us taking a job, but we had put so much focus on customer service, neither of us felt that we could keep that momentum by substituting a key player. The number of hours we were already putting in for the shop allowed little time to make moonlighting a viable option. Nothing short of a miracle would turn this thing around.

And yet, I was getting this increased sense of calm. There were longer periods between panic attacks. In an effort to understand the clairaudient experience that marked my descent down the rabbit hole, I added spiritually themed books to the one hour of reading time I set aside to review business information. Then I began to read spiritually based *business* books. Inspired by what I was reading and curious to see the possible results, I added 15 minutes of meditation to my daily routine as a means of centering me for the day.

Mike had begun to read many of the same books I was reading. "Spiritual growth" was something for which we had a frame of reference, but never a strong desire to explore — or so we thought. But it was becoming clear to both of us that this was a path we were walking together. It was in fact perfectly captured in my journal entry of October 17, 2007, as a simple statement. Shortly after the *Sacred Fire* project was begun, and the record business loss was entered on the books, I wrote: "I desire to be free from fear with a peaceful mind."

Later, as I prepared notes about "loving service" and "the fear/love continuum" for a book I was working on, I would be revisited by the last two lines of the song: *as a servant you're more free than ever, with a mastery over your fear.*

My "simple" request for a peaceful mind in October 2007 had become the first of two declarations that would change my life forever. By the time the album went to press in October 2008, I could no longer deny that the song, as well as the entire line-up of the album, was beginning to take on a spiritual, if not magical, quality. The whole project had returned something to me that desired to *live*, to be healthy — to find answers in the best and most complete way I knew how.

As dramatic as it seemed, it felt like the *Sacred Fire* project had saved my life...or handed me a new one.

In the illumination afforded me by my own sacred fire, I began to understand: if my business was going to fail, all of the gut-wrenching, heart-stopping, paralytic fear in the world was not going to stop the failure — and may in fact kill me. At the very least it would set the stage for a whole host of problems. And if the business managed to be a success...

Well I better darn well learn how to enjoy it!

I was starting to listen to my intuition. And what it told me was that I needed to take responsibility for my emotions and to understand the role that responsibility played in the success of the business and music as well. I had to be truthful with myself that I wasn't always authentic in my expression of gratitude for my gifts and talents. I had a husband who loved me dearly — but how much could I return that love when I was less than loving with myself? At times I lacked courage, and looked to others to provide it for me, but I was the only one who could change this. I began to surrender more often and allow things to just "show up" for me in music, without attaching them to a specific outcome or gain.

One of the many unexpected outcomes related to music "showed up" during a charity event and wine tasting we attended in connection with our shop. I struck up a conversation with a writer who was beginning an online radio network that would be spiritually based. When he discovered that I was a musician recording my fourth CD, he asked if I would be interested in doing the music program for his network. It would be a wonderful opportunity to plug a new album, and I could freely promote myself as the owner of the shop with airtime that didn't cost anything.

I said yes.

In June of 2008 I launched the first episode of *Music and The Muse*. By September of the same year, I and two of the other hosts left to form our own network; and the program expanded to interview a number of people whose books I had read. I now had the privilege of asking my questions in person. The program, *Passion's Purpose*, had a spiritually based format and featured people who were making a difference with the expression of their innate gifts.

Another unexpected outcome to "show up" arrived in the form of a guest brought by a friend to the *Sacred Fire* CD release party. She was an art collector *and* an angel investor. Upon sharing that I had created a franchise plan for the shop she expressed an interest in reviewing it. I agreed to furnish her with the executive summary for that plan within a week.

I now had what seemed like my miracle.

By late November of 2008 I found myself back in a conversation with my friend Susan.

"I feel really good, Suz—both physically and mentally. I'm starting to think I may pull this business thing together yet. Between the course I took to write proposals for the federal government—which looks like it will put us back in the black on a regular basis—and the loan that I applied for based on our credit score which will reduce our interest, I can actually see this thing working. Franchising the frame shop and gallery: that's HUGE. I am starting to see real wealth attached to this."

"I don't think the gallery is going to make you rich," she countered. There was that word again. I gulped hard as I recognized the intensity in her eyes—a twin to that look she'd given me in the parking lot over a year ago. It seemed to be present more and more, especially when she had a point to make that was prophetic.

"But at the same time I think you need to be here now..." she continued. "If you look at everything you are doing, it seems that the shop *is* leading you to your destiny, which I still think is your music."

Then her gaze became extremely focused as she leaned in to make her point. "Nan, you still don't understand how your songs affect people, or how important they are. The shop has taught you many things about business, beyond what you already knew, but it has also led you to other things...things that put you in a radio program and took you back to recording and performing again. It could be that this business offers a time bridge to let your music be understood and fully appreciated. The fact is, there's a right time for everything."

That was a lot to absorb; and there were so many ways that I could have responded—questioned—discussed. But after a moment's silence there was only one truth that found a voice.

"It just feels good not to be so afraid anymore."

# Sacred Fire Boarding Pass

PERMISSION · GRANTED · TO · COME · ABOARD

Notes

Journal Entries

# Chapter Seven

## Because of the Effect

*"In Adrianna's dream such joy is found in song,
in the eventide she playfully hides until she's coaxed along
by the ones who call her name, to hear of magic tales..."*
...from Adrianna's Dream, *song lyrics*
*- Adrianna Larkin -*


Susan wasn't willing to let the point be dropped. "Suz, I know you love the music, and that means a lot to me; but I think you may be giving it greater importance than it deserves. I have a chance to really make something here, and it's unnerving to hear you say that it might not work."

"It has nothing to do with me loving your music — but of course I do...I just know that you have a gift, a *real* gift. And I can't help but feel that the shop is simply a 'spacer' for the right timing of that gift."

"You're certainly smart enough to pull off a franchise plan. It's brilliant — and the fact that you have an investor interested speaks to that. An art and framing franchise designed to self-perpetuate its own market by fostering a return of societal engagement with the arts — who thinks along those lines? *You* do—but I still feel the shop is only temporary—if based on nothing else than the number of people who go out of their way after one of your performances to tell you how much the songs mean to them."

I had to agree with her, if only silently. Even in the presence of self doubt, I couldn't deny it. Although it seemed odd at times, I recalled so many instances of someone's poignant connection to my music. Some of the more memorable included the 17-year old college student who stared at me with disbelief after I'd performed *The Only One* at a gathering of friends.

The song was drawn from my life as a single parent, and from the first few lines it had created a steady stream of tears down the young girl's face. She was choking back sobs as she approached me. "Oh my God, I get it now. I was raised by a single mom and I never understood what she meant when she said I helped raise her as much as she raised me…now I do."

Then there was the restaurant patron, a lady with severe Alzheimer's who regularly dined with her husband…but she never spoke intelligibly…she never remembered his name. The first night I performed there she carried on an extensive and clear conversation with me during my break—about what she found enjoyable in music, about what she found enjoyable in mine.

Science and medicine aside, it was as if something in the songs temporarily reconnected the circuits in her brain.

Unexpected responses of this nature were frequent and occurred with almost every performance where I had personal contact with the crowd thereafter. Going back to the days of working in the emergency room, I would often sing to myself as I stocked shelves. Unintended audiences were everywhere, and on more than one occasion I had patients ask that I sing to them.

Children seemed especially taken with my songs. It became a common occurrence to have a child between the ages of 2 and 5 break free from his mother's hand and join me on stage. I had never really paused to consider this Pied Piper effect I had on the pre-school set.

Once a 20-something man offered an effusive commentary after listening to another original song, *When She's Lonely*. He needed to share how moved he'd been, that he felt the song was a message to men as well as women to avoid sabotaging their relationships with their careers.

Sometimes people heard things in the music that I had never intended to be there, yet spurred them to have these emotive experiences. And sometimes the experiences were something that fell just short of mass hysteria. The one I found to be most unusual occurred at the stage production from my first performance with Mae Wheeler. We would laugh about it many years later.

"Girl...that was something else. There were 18 Divas and the best of the best in Gospel, Jazz, Soul, and Blues...and you...*you*...got the only standing ovation!" I had argued with her when she first brought it up, and continued to do so until I reviewed the videotape to see for myself.

What I saw completely knocked me over.

This had been another one of those nerve-wracking events. I was the folk/country contingent in an audience that was primarily African-American. My soft, dulcet flower-child tones followed the power of the first soprano of the St. Louis Opera, literally redefining *a hard act to follow*. I could not possibly feel smaller, more outclassed, and rendered nearly invisible by the wide range of voices who commanded large audiences on their names alone. It was my first time on a national stage.

I stepped out in my backless full-length formal to the mixed curse and blessing of The Westport Playhouse revolving stage—a feature for which it was very well known. It would be understatement to say that this provided an interesting sensation, and a good deal of diversion from my stage fright, as it offered the additional challenge to remain vertical while balancing on rarely worn stiletto heels.

Mae had her usual A-list of musicians to back up the divas, and there had been rehearsals for all songs to be performed that evening. But with my original compositions no one would know what I was playing, so I brought in Dave Black. It was the first time we would share a stage as I performed songs from my debut album. I had made the decision not to accompany myself as I did not feel that the formal, the heels, the guitar, and the stage were things I wanted to negotiate simultaneously. As I walked up to the microphone and the stage began to turn, I commended myself on such a brilliant decision.

Still, not having a guitar made me a bit at a loss as to what to do with my hands. As I got into the music, I found my body's natural rhythm. All of it. But mostly that in my arms. Rather uniquely I might add, because the video revealed my gestures to have an uncanny resemblance to The Chicken Dance that you see performed at weddings with sufficient quantities of alcohol.

These gestures that would most likely be performed by a poultry-human hybrid were soon picked up on by the musicians from the previous act who had not exited the stage. Most of them had put their instruments down, but they remained on stage at polite attention for the next performer. With gestures that appeared to be unconsciously linked to my own, it wasn't long before we were all "flapping in formalwear." The keyboard player picked up the tune, its key and meter, and added to the feeling of festivity. The audience picked up on this impromptu musical, and physical, jam session and "joined in the flap" as it were.

"It's like I told you," Mae would remind me time and again, "it doesn't matter how *you* think you did, it matters how *they* think you did...and you got a standing ovation."

By late December of 2008, the business woman half of me was already aware that I would be writing a record number of commercial proposals come January. We had bid on a government contract that would equal sales for the last two months of our busiest season—Christmas—which would start our first quarter profits off nicely. Additionally, we had yet more assurance that the financing we had applied for would go through as our credit score had remained quite good. The icing on the cake was the interest displayed by the angel investor.

It finally felt like we had turned the corner.

I had picked up a book whose title was tossed around at one of my networking groups—*Spiritual Selling* (John Wiley & Sons, Inc., 2007), written by Joe Nunziata (www.jnunziata.com). I enjoyed his work as it offered good information for balance in business, and I knew I would equally enjoy having a conversation with him on the air. Scheduling guests whose books I already read had two major benefits: it lessened the amount of prep time before a show, and I had the distinct advantage of having my questions personally answered. When his name came up again through another radio contact, I knew enough to consider it a sign.

An on-air conversation led to a working relationship which in turn would result in the second important declaration I would make in March of 2009:

That I was a singer/songwriter.

By this time I could not deny that the latest CD, *Sacred Fire,* was linked to my metamorphosis and carried with it some intense spiritual vibration. It really was an anthem for the emergence of something I was only beginning to understand.

After declaring my purpose, I had followed with this intent:

*And I trust that the exit from the business will take place in the quickest, easiest, and most appropriate way for me.*

I had made peace with the fact that the franchise would take some time to develop and I might have to remain with it longer than I originally intended. I knew that the Universe would find a way to make all the puzzle pieces fit. It always did. I didn't know yet how that would relate to my expressed declarations or intention, but I looked forward to watching it all unfold—in whatever way that was to happen.

Still I wondered…what *would* all of that look like?

The question received an unanticipated response in the collapse of the banking industry.

# Chapter Eight

The Clearing

*"Dreams we believed were forever
are now gone in the next breath we take...
Time has brought us this far, it will take us the rest of the way..."
...from* Time Has Brought, *song lyrics*
- Adrianna Larkin -

In February of 2009 the bailouts for the banks had begun. The record number of commercial bids I had written for the first two months of 2009 seemed to be on terminal hold. None of my customers had their budgets in place—or the budgets that remained in place were drastically reduced. I communicated with the lender whose package guaranteed my financing based on my credit score. "We can't get anything through, not for you, not for anyone—at this rate we'll *all* be flipping burgers in a few weeks." His distress was palpable.

The large government contract that on its own would have equaled our last two months of sales had a target time frame for delivery by early February. Weeks after the deadline for its completion, it had not been awarded to anyone either. A new president had taken office and awards that required custom framing were put on the back burner in the company of many other purchases, as they were reviewed to determine expenditure necessity.

The investor who had previously been so enthusiastic about the executive summary now called to advise that she would not be able to help at this time. She let it be known that she had recently lost several hundred thousand dollars in a property sale; and reading between the lines I assumed that the market drop was taking its toll on a number of resources also.

By late spring the credit lines were cut. The one card that did not cut its credit line raised the APR to 37% in spite of the fact I had not missed a payment, had never been late. I called them to ask if this was a mistake. The others raised their rates as well. "Do you show me as being delinquent, late, anything?" I asked.

"No ma'am, you have a history of timely payment on this account..."

I cut her off, "Then why..."

"We have reviewed your account and feel it to be appropriate at this time."

We held out hope in late spring and early summer as we spoke with people who discussed buying the business as it was — perhaps we could just break even. I would offer the franchise plan, the resources I had created, all the intellectual property which was significant, and several parties stepped forward with interest. They simply couldn't get their own financing in place.

At the same time that the business was working through a series of challenges, music was offering more opportunities. I received and accepted an offer to perform with a global festival in Long Beach, California. *Live H2O,*

*The Concert of the Living Water*, was scheduled to take place the weekend of June 21, 2009 in a number of cities across the globe. My invitation had come from Al Diaz (*www*.ilumine-ao.com), author of *The Titus Concept* (Morgan James Publishing, LLC 2005) who was on the committee to help organize the Long Beach festival site. The attendance was expected to be anywhere from 5,000 to 10,000 people. That seemed plausible due to its proximity to Los Angeles and the draw of their keynote speaker Dr. Masura Emoto, whose work was referenced in the movie *What the Bleep Do We Know?!*

Al Diaz also hosted a program on Blogtalkradio and we had become friends. As a big fan of the *Sacred Fire* song, he had shared the entire album with the committee; and I was invited to be listed with the other performers. He asked if I could be joined by the band to perform at the concert.

The availability of the musicians along with the plan to broadcast all performances globally — including mine — made this a very attractive prospect. The information I received in the planning stage was that only the Maui and Long Beach sites would have the live streaming twenty-four hour coverage. Global exposure for my music was very possible, and if indeed there were resources that could come from music that would place me where I wanted to be, then maybe we could clear our obligations with the shop and just go forward.

Since my own background included a certain amount of event planning, I wasn't surprised at the subsequent outcome that occurred as the result of the economy and loss of volunteer staff. Upon my arrival in Long Beach, I learned that funding had not been received as anticipated. Volunteers were stretched thin, and the core group of about 20 or so that was counted on to be the lifeblood of the operation had been reduced to less than half that. Few of the events received the video, and Mike and I noted the attendance to be less than 1,000 people each day.

I recalled my experience one month after 9/11 on a visit to a B&B in a normally well trafficked resort town. It had appeared nearly deserted. Not lightly attended, but *deserted*. Talking with the owners and shopkeepers who relied on this traffic for their very survival, few were just barely able to hang on. The media was still full throttle with the daily doom and gloom report. It no longer seemed to bear any relationship to the tragedy itself—that was already "old news"—but had shifted focus to the *what ifs,* milking the horror of that single day in the hopes that it would provide endless fodder to feed the paralyzing fear that kept people home and glued to their television sets.

The same climate of fear was being broadcast daily in June of 2009 with reckless abandon. Market trends, a new president, bank bailouts, corporate corruption, were all subject to *extreme* magnification in their analysis. Although not as riveting—or perhaps personally impacting—as 9/11, the fear mongers had to make do with what they could. Desperate times call for desperate measures.

On Sunday, June 21, 2009, I performed with a 4-person band on a stage in the sand—to a good number less than I anticipated. I would have been happy with a few hundred in the audience.

I think we had 12.

As I loaded up instruments to take back to the car, one of the attendees in the audience, a petite woman I estimated to be in her late 50s, was keeping stride with the brisk gait I had in an effort to get everything packed up and in the car that was parked a good distance away.

"I wanted to let you know how much I enjoyed your

music," she said. I wondered if she knew how much I appreciated her at that time. I slowed just enough to take in her face that was genuine in its enthusiasm.

She went on as she walked nearly the whole distance to the parking lot. "This is so unfair…they have four stages going at the same time—none of the talent has a great attendance because it is all so spread out and each act is competing with the next one. I just think that everyone on this beach needed to hear *you* and your music…you were *wonderful!*"

Three of the four band members headed for the airport, but Mike and I had decided not to fly out until the next day. Benet, the drummer, had decided to remain an additional day as well to catch up with a friend who lived in the area. We already planned to give him a ride to Venice Beach where they were to connect. A brief stop for the indulgence of Margaritas got a unanimous vote as he had some time to pass before his friend would be off work.

There had been less time to converse with Benet than any member of the group. He remained very busy, booking other acts and performing regularly as key player in more than one band. Most of the time, the venues I had performed in were smaller or could not accommodate drums; and, except for the CD release, the only other appearance he had been a part of was a charity concert featuring the same group of players one month before Long Beach.

In the instant replay of the performance that followed, I felt obligated to apologize for what I felt reflected my own lack of skill as a musician. As I dissected my performance and noted the areas that needed to be improved, like timing, transitions, and remembering the changes in the bridge of the arrangements, he offered his point of view:

"Nan, everything you just mentioned as 'a problem' is completely correctable with playing out more. It's all practice. And if you think about it, we've only performed together as a group two times...I don't even count the CD release party because that was so brief. You have surrounded yourself with some top notch players..."

"That was no accident," I interrupted.

"I know...I do the same thing. I can't get enough stage time with someone like Tom Maloney. He has the ability to go from the macroscopic to the microscopic in his performance of music, and I always learn something from him. Playing with people who have more skill in some areas is how *we* get to be stronger—they become our teachers..."

And I completely understood the instruction I was receiving at that moment. I had sought to be better, and better, and better still. Always evolving, always growing, never comfortable in resting at a new level of skill. I wanted to develop my voice, my phrasing, my stage presence, my writing style—and to a limited degree, skill on the guitar. This last category had been secondary to everything else as I could rely on another guitar player, but only I could "deliver the goods" for my own performance. I was forever hungry for what other talents could teach me, but this had created a sense of always being a student and never a master.

I was suddenly aware that I had mistakenly related the status of "student" as being equal to the status of "unskilled."

On the return flight home, I had a lot of time to think about how everything had unfolded. The concert had not brought the national exposure that I had hoped for, but gave me something else. Something perhaps that I needed much more: an ability to get a clear assessment of what my strengths and weaknesses really were.

And the shop was looking more and more like it was landing in the "weakness" category.

Home again, the focus rapidly shifted from our brief time in the performance arena to the next step of the business. We held onto the remaining potential of two buyers. One of them, researched extensively, turned out to be fraudulent. The other, although extremely interested, reported that financing was out of the question.

Finally, after the last potential buyer threw in the towel, we began the process for Chapter 7. The shop would close just one month before celebrating our fifth year in business. We would declare personal bankruptcy because of the amount of assets we had committed to the business. This included our home, which would go back to the bank as well.

Mike retained his usual buoyant approach. "It's all a great adventure, babe."

"That's what I get for encouraging you to read along with me," I quipped. Though Mike always took things in stride a good deal more than I did, he had undergone his transformation that lined up perfectly with my own. In sharing with him the books that I had acquired to better understand and "heal" myself, we landed in many discussions about what applied to each of us and what did not. The discussions had a side benefit of removing limitations that he recognized for himself. What remained underneath it all was a greater emphasis of his Zen-like view that everything had a purpose.

And it seemed too well timed to deny: My expressed desire to exit the business in the quickest way possible seemed undeniably linked to the declaration of myself as a musician and my intent to have that happen as soon as possible.

Had we sold the business, there most likely would not be clearing to move on, especially if the franchise plan were picked up with any part of it. Some part, be it physical or emotional, would always have remained attached. I could not possibly have removed myself from any degree of business success that my father and grandfather had been fated to be denied.

And in the heat of any sale, I would have no time allowed for music.

I had been terrified of watching it all crumble, and on the surface that seemed to be exactly what was taking place. I had lost my business, my means of regular employment, my extra vehicle, and would soon surrender my home.

But I had recovered my health, my own sacred fire, and the support of a partner who adored me — all in addition to having my request fulfilled for a peaceful mind. I recovered joy as I renewed my connections with offspring. I had received the unsolicited support of friends, family, associates, and strangers in ways I never thought possible. I was well fed, sheltered, and warmly clothed. All my essential needs were met. I now had the opportunity, with no holds barred, to jump into the life that I had tried for so many years to throw under the bus — that of a singer/songwriter. All that remained now was for me to accept one thing:

That I really had become rich beyond my wildest dreams — and the wealth was so much more than I had imagined.

I had accepted the invitation to my right purpose, and what showed up as my prosperity was virtually invisible to the naked eye — that is to anyone but me. There was no mansion here. No bank account with several digits and commas representing the balance. In fact, any and all material means were dissolving rapidly....

But I had reached the core of my true wealth: *my feeling*. It was the only stock I owned, but I would never have to surrender it — and its value was destined to increase.

I had remembered reading so many stories about people with seemingly unlimited physical wealth whose lives were marred by misery or the fear of losing it all. But I had gained the understanding of the main point offered by Buddha: It is not the things that happen to us that cause our suffering...

It is how we feel about them.

Filing a Chapter 7 bankruptcy was not something I found enjoyable, but I made peace with it. I had come to view it for what it was: a necessary step of clearing and the integral piece that was needed in order to move forward.

Now there was just one question that remained:

Why music?

What was it about the music that seemed to engage so many people? I felt the last tiny remnant of doubt could be addressed if I just had this one answer.

As I made a practice of meditation daily, I turned to this to provide the answer to my question. My meditation had become a pattern, often taking me to a place that I recognized as a temple. There to greet me at the door was a small, frail looking monk who would sit across from me on the floor. Sometimes he would speak, often he didn't. A few times I could remember the advice he had given me, but if my conscious mind could not recall it, I knew that in our time together I had received something that would be there when I needed it most.

On this one particular morning chosen to ponder the question of the music, I had knocked on the door of the temple. The door opened. The person on the other side was not the monk...

It was me.

I recognized the "me" on the other side of the door as my Higher Self. Although my body looked essentially the same, it was a little trimmer, healthier, more radiant, glowing.

It was me without my baggage.

"I've been waiting for you," she said. Her expectancy was pure joy and radiance. Not unlike that of a child waiting on Santa with the same amount of anticipation, knowing that the hour of my arrival was near. I could sense her feelings and I could sense my own, separate yet simultaneous, as I watched the two of us together in the same space from the vantage point of being in the audience. In the course of the ensuing dialogue—enough to craft another book—I posed the question.

"What is it that seems to make people want to listen to me?"

"Sacred geometry," came the brief reply, punctuated with the bonus of a smile.

"What...what about it?"

"Look it up."

"You can't explain it to me?" I challenged.

"I could...but if I did you wouldn't believe me. You

still don't completely trust your own instincts. That is why you are here. And this whole experience is freaking you out a little bit. There is a part of you that wants to think of this as just a crazy lucid dream. Nan, honey, I have always been here for you, *you just didn't always have the means to hear me...*"

Suddenly I knew the source of my clairaudient experience. I had been talking to myself — *at the level of the soul*. The crafting of *Sacred Fire*, in the musical as well as metaphorical sense, offered an amplification system for the guidance being received from this very source.

My Higher Self continued: "If you take the time to research it, you will find a relationship of your music to sacred geometry that you can accept as valid."

"Besides," she added with an even bigger smile, "you'll appreciate it more this way."

My higher self delighted greatly in this last response. It was the same line I always used on my son when helping him with homework.

I did as my soul directed: a search for sacred geometry brought descriptions involving architecture, and nature — and, of course, mathematics. I already knew those. Finally, I found the reference to music.

I read the text: "Sacred Geometry in music is believed to be produced with the third and fifth harmonic." My mouth fell open. I instantly had my answer. Since the early days of playing guitar, I held a deep-rooted fear that all my songs would sound the same. It was one thing to beat the drum of a certain feeling. It was something else entirely to do it with the same droning melody line.

What I viewed as my limited skill — often the source of my insecurity — had caused me to purposefully craft different combinations in an effort to give variety to the music through means other than the obvious technical skill that I felt I lacked. For that reason, I found it easiest to compose the music using the root chord and sing the melody line at the *third or fifth harmonic*. *The sacred geometry had been formed in the chord that appeared between the voice and the song.*

When another meditation yielded yet another meeting with Higher Self, I asked, "Do I write about all this?"

Higher Self flashed her toothy grin, one that I recognized as my own during moments when I was really pleased with myself.

"What do you think?" came her reply.

"Maybe — yes — when the time is right," I nodded.

"Good answer," she replied.

I wasn't certain when that would be, when that "time is right" would surface. But I knew beyond any doubt that the timing would make itself clear — and trust was all that I needed until then.

# Chapter Nine

## Welcome Home

*"Within the walls of a little house, I would not ask for very much,*
*A quiet smile and a tender touch, to know I have come home,*
*Love will hang its hat in here, I know my time is drawing near,*
*To this inviting atmosphere I will soon call home..."*
*...from* Coming Home, *song lyrics*
*- Adrianna Larkin -*

The tone of my story was purposely designed to read more like a work of fiction than actual experience. But I can assure you: it is all real. I chose this approach because our memory for stories is often much longer than the memory we have for factual accounts (and there will be things from my tale that will be helpful to remember as we go forward). That perspective is just one of perhaps several unusual features of this book.

Another is that the book begins in the middle of the story. The first draft was being completed while I was building a full-time music career and the bankruptcy was being finalized. Mine isn't a story that has been colored by distance. I have read those accounts. They afford a certain amount of reassurance that you can come through any ordeal with a passage of time and even have it wind up to be the next "rags to riches" encounter.

While there is nothing wrong with that, if you are like me you remain a mere mortal who still must wrestle with a crisis of faith from time to time with your own story. When our faith is challenged it is hard to believe that we can endure long enough to hang in there today — let alone come through on the other side after weeks or months of trial.

What I offer is coming to you in real time — or as close to that as is possible in a book. It is not a tale told from the other side but from a reference point that I think is the same position held by many people who experience a desire for reinvention: How do I get from where I am to where I want to be?

Now having said all that, you probably think you've just hired a tour guide who has never even been to the city. I can't blame you — it certainly could appear that way. Please trust me when I say that the reason I am absolutely positive *I* can get there — and you can too — is because of an awareness I did not have at the start of my story:

*We have already been here before.*

Re-inventing ourselves is not new. If you have ever held more than one job (even in the same industry), moved to a new town, gotten married, had kids, started a new hobby, you have re-invented yourself many times over.

What may be new in this instance — what may prove to be the greatest challenge — is:

- Although you know what you want, you believe it cannot be done with your present circumstances.
- You are still unclear as to what you wish to do; and

without clear vision, any possibility for re-invention seems non-existent.

Have you ever visited a town that you once knew so well but returned after a period of time to feel utterly disoriented? The new construction, road signs, addition of streets can make it seem as though you have never been there before.

Whether you know it or not, your own "infrastructure" has undergone the same kind of additions and reconstruction. With the passing of years, the ordinary becomes the extraordinary. You have branched out into new experiences, acquired new skills and knowledge. And because all of this has occurred so gradually to change your surroundings, any look inward to find a safe and familiar skyline instead reflects a completely alien landscape.

The people who seem to make it look so easy to pick up and move, change careers, turn a hobby into a livelihood, become a success with the odds stacked against them, or anything else that spells a reinvention, all have one thing in common: they have refined the process of self-examination and taken stock of their assets acquired with the passage of time.

Like someone who gains familiarity with a new city, they have learned where the hospital is in case of emergency and they have already scoped out the location of the best park or museum. They can handle a detour on a different route home because they already know where their favorite band will be in concert later that night.

If that seems overly simplistic, think of it another way: how many of us would consciously choose to live without those skills we have taken the time to acquire for use in daily life, whether that is searching the internet, dialing a telephone, driving a car or operating a lawn mower? Everything we have learned, and the tools we have acquired, even if we are not aware that we have them, are now assets. The secret is first to know that you *have* assets, then learn how to leverage them to obtain the life of your dreams.

## Resilience with Resources

By the time I was 30 (over 20 years ago), I was already convinced that the resilience I had in my 20s was greatly diminished with the emergence of my third decade. In my 20s everything seemed larger than life. Changes for which I had no frame of reference — my first marriage, a child, a new career — seemed huge and extremely dramatic. Yet at the same time I had a feeling that even with the unexpected challenges, I had the ability to bounce back and land on my feet with ease.

By the time I had reached my mid-thirties (and second divorce), it felt as though there was a lot less bounce. Yet whatever I had lost in that department had been replaced by *experience*. I used to think that the *resources* provided by experience were gifted to us in exchange for the *resilience* we had to surrender in our youth. I have since revised that theory.

I feel we still have both.

The reason we often don't feel as resilient as we once did is simply this: *We are not placing ourselves in the rapidly changing and often <u>risky</u> environment that we once did in order to arrive at a destination.*

As an example, I waited almost six years between the

first and second marriage. Having a small child to raise and working on my bachelor's degree, I wasn't eager to rush into something that would complicate and possibly jeopardize either one of those. Does that make me less resilient? I don't think so. Just more thoughtful.

Those of us who spend a lot of time planning, preparing, structuring our lives for the best possible outcome are some of the most challenged when it comes to figuring out what we want, or taking the bold leap of faith needed to get there.

But here's the flip side: if we can get out of our own way, we also have the highest degree of success. Whether we recognize it or not, the use of our skills and abilities in concert with a degree of planning and preparation leverages our resources perfectly.

And that is exactly what we had to do each time we re-invented ourselves whether out of necessity (for a new job) or out of desire (for a family with children).

Re-invention for our heart's desire is really just *change*...although at times it feels like change on steroids. That's understandable. When we are forced, or choose, to look inward, we're welcomed back to that strange new city that we may have been away from for a very long time. For some, they may not remember *ever* taking in that skyline. If that's the case, they may move a little slower in finding their true north and safely navigating foreign geography.

Be it strange or be it change—it can still be scary.

## Fear:  Another Kind of "F" Word

My earliest understanding of love and fear being oppositional came to me as I read *Conversations with God* (Hampton Roads Publishing, 2005) by Neale Donald Walsch.

I, like so many other people, always believed the opposite of love is hate. It was only after reading this book that I really started to understand that *hate* may be the symptom, but *fear is the disease.*

"Hate" that shows up in the form of bigotry, gang wars, and crime, stems from the same source as the discomfort felt in a toxic relationship. All is fueled by fear which comes from a lack of knowledge of how to make things different. Fear will also keep us stuck in a climate of unrest. Subsequently, I can agree with Mr. Walsch's presentation that fear is the one true devil.

I have heard psychologists and spiritual experts reference that where we are in our satisfaction with life can be plotted on a continuum with fear at one end and love at the other. In my mind, it looks simply like this:

Dissatisfied                                                    Satisfied

----------------------------------------------------------------------------

FEAR                                                               LOVE

The degree of happiness and satisfaction and that point of where you are—be it to the left or to the right—on that same scale will largely predict the comfort that you have with any process of reinvention.

For those of you finding yourself newly unemployed, outside of the relationship that you came to rely on, or any number of things that are suddenly unfamiliar to you, moving toward the fear end of the scale is natural. For reasons that I will discuss in other chapters, it can be a necessary place to visit, but trust me: you don't want to live here.

And that is where sacred fire comes in. It is the spark of enthusiasm born out of falling in love with your true

90

purpose (even if that purpose seems a little out of focus) that can keep you moving forward toward the right side of the scale.

And why should our reinvention be forthcoming with true purpose? Because that purpose has the potential to make the quantum leap from the left side of the scale as it is the only thing completely comprised of love: a love which will so fully occupy the space that if fear enters it cannot remain for long before being squeezed out. Once you enter into the space of true purpose, what you find there may be completely unexpected.

As I was preparing to write about my own story, sacred fire demonstrated that it still had more surprises in store. Seeking to pick up some extra work to supplement the performance, I applied to talent agencies for voiceover work. Feedback from the radio program had encouraged me to inquire about being a "behind the scenes" announcer for television and radio spots. I applied at two talent agencies. The second agency who signed me became very excited about my background, but not for the reasons I had considered.

It seems that in an industry that is loaded with teen applicants desiring to be the next *Top Model* or parents seeking a career for their offspring as a child star, there is a current shortage of 40+ folks to play doctors, lawyers, and assorted other business professionals. I agreed to join a casting call attended by approximately 40 other people. In a room where I appeared to be the only one past the age of 25 — I had just celebrated my 51st birthday — I ran through all the paces that seemed to have very little to do with voiceover talent.

At the end of the exercise, we were advised as a group to call in on Monday to see if we made the cut. I didn't see how anything related to voice could translate to my "walk across stage" and taping that day, but I called in just out of curiosity to see where I was.

"You know, we see a lot of people and you should understand that we choose very few." I was already prepping for the pitch that would let me down easy, accompanied by the "try again next time" speech.

"We are very interested and would like you to come on board," is the message that was delivered instead.

After a careful review of the contract and a sufficient amount of questioning and due diligence, I signed and now here I am: right back where I started from.

A week later I had a music audition for a steady performance gig in a club and noted that something had changed. I was tired, a little hoarse, and even with a fair amount of ability to work around these things, I still knew I was not at the top of my game. This alone would have sent me into orbit once upon a time, but I noticed that I felt different. I was comfortable in my own skin and what I could do.

It seemed that in finding the courage to reconnect with that initial sacred fire felt so long ago, I had flavored everything else with just the right amount of seasoning. I finally got out of my own way to cease doing damage control—which really only created the damage I was trying to avoid in the first place.

If my own journey had been intentional I may have stumbled less with introductions along the way. And because of that, I want yours to be an easier one...to know that these pages will give you the opportunity to shake hands with many strangers that you think you may not have met before or can't recognize because it has been so long:

- Your own purpose
- Your own skills and attributes
- Your own dreams and desires
- Your personality
- Your own divinity

And even if you feel like a stranger in a strange land, I hope you can trust me when I say that you *have* been here before — and that is exactly why you can get there again.

# Sacred Fire Boarding Pass

PERMISSION·GRANTED·TO·COME·ABOARD

Notes
_____
Journal Entries

# Chapter Ten

·͜ʃͶͶͶͶͶ·

## The Proof is in the Feeling

*"But if you feel a little bad, and you can get a little sad*
*There is no need to get too mad at the cards life would deal ya'..."*
*...from* You Can't Sing the Blues (in a Sushi Bar), *song lyrics*
*- Adrianna Larkin -*

Depending on which poll you review, between 70-80% of people in the American workforce today have some element of dissatisfaction with their current employment. What does that have to do with igniting a sacred fire?

Everything.

If you ask people why they remain at jobs they are not excited about going to in the morning, nearly everyone would say they need the money. It is ironic then that when people leave one place of employment for another, money is seldom ever cited as the reason.

People may seek a better position, better hours, better benefits, more vacation time, more respect, or a different type of work. Sometimes it is because they do not wish to uproot their families. All these things unrelated to money will be more likely to have someone risk newness (and another reinvention) far more often than better pay. The truth is: *we seldom ever leave a tolerable work situation for money alone.*

Several sources exist to tell us: it's not about the "money"-- it's about the "happy."

- In a 2009 survey performed by the Society for Human Resource Management, only 30% of workers polled reported that they were *very* satisfied with their pay.

- Assuming that 70% of the workforce lacks satisfaction with their wages, it seems yet more curious that an online survey conducted by *Right Management* reported only 18% of people leaving their jobs for better benefits or pay. (Of the 11 reasons given, this ranked as number seven in order of priority.)

- A study performed by Ran Kivetz and Anat Keinan of Columbia University, as reported by Robin Lloyd for LiveScience (August 2006) revealed that the guilt experienced over self-indulgent practices will pass as quickly as it appears; but regrets over missed opportunities actually *increase* with time.

In spite of all the signs pointing to the factors that we should pay attention to regarding how we *feel* about our work — satisfied or dissatisfied (love vs. fear) — we still look to external things like money as being the reason to remain where we are.

Imagine the power that could exist then, if we chose

to use that same *feeling* to guide our process for our own reinvention.

## Intuition, it's Not Just for "Woo-Woo" Anymore

I need to make a case for intuition because I believe it's an integral part of the human experience — whether we choose to acknowledge that or not. When we were young, before language was a tool we used regularly for communication, we looked to the expressions of our caregivers and monitored the climate of emotion displayed by those around us to choose what our next action would be.

Intuition at its core is simply the acknowledgement of our feelings. It can be one of the most valuable tools at your disposal. In addition, it can lead you to many really nice things.

There are varying degrees of comfort around the word intuition and probably just as many definitions in our society. Just for fun (and as a starting point) I pulled my old Funk & Wagnall Dictionary from the bookshelf, and noticed that it had two possible choices to offer:

1. The power or faculty of knowing things without conscious reasoning
2. Quick and ready insight

The part about "without conscious reasoning" from the first definition best illustrates the point I made earlier about changing jobs for reasons other than money. It also gives me the chance to form my own definition: Intuition is a conclusion based on how you <u>feel</u> rather than what you <u>think</u>.

Thinking is rampant. We do it by default. In fact,

most modern career and lifestyle choices have an ever-increasing amount of processes that require our thinking as the entryway into the business of day to day living.

Filling out tax forms, applying for student loans, paying the mortgage, planning a vacation, even getting kids ready for school requires a runaway train of thought that seems to go on forever and makes it difficult to shut down the mind or even to go to sleep at night. All this *thinking* can leave almost no room for *feeling*.

And let's face it: there are some feelings that seem just too scary to acknowledge in any way.

When it comes to things like childhood traumas, a broken heart, the sense of betrayal after losing one's job, "feeling" seems to be the last choice we would make. Running away from it may even seem the only one that *could* be made. The last thing we want to hear is someone telling us to face those monsters and allow ourselves to *feel*. But acknowledging those feelings and giving yourself the permission to be angry, sad, or even frightened is necessary to get to the other side.

Not long ago, I was having a conversation with a friend who knew of my conflict with my Dad over the desire to be an actress (and the resulting anger I carried for many years after). Although I thought I had worked through those things, he suggested--being rather intuitive himself—that there were still some unresolved feelings.

I really wanted to deny it (and in fact I did for a time) but committed to my own growth as I was, I had to examine if what he said *felt* like it had any truth at all. When I realized he *could* be right, I started going back—further than my teens when I thought our conflict began, to my earliest childhood memory.

It seems in that time I called up a memory of my dad

trying to teach me to tell time, and losing patience because I could not understand what he was saying. I was about four years of age. The more I tried to clarify what I wanted to know, the more he took it as a challenge to his ability to teach. It escalated to me crying and him yelling over my tearful protest to the point where my mother interceded. I was told to go play, after which some words were no doubt exchanged between my parents.

And what was the value of feeling all this after so much time had passed? Surprisingly, I felt a lightness afterwards that I did not expect to have.

We tend to think that our feelings have to be "big" and somehow "justified" in order to feel them, but even the smallest of things can leave their mark. The more we tend to ignore the way we feel, the more likely we are to suppress those feelings until they begin to block all movement forward or we try to numb them with addictions like food, alcohol, or our work.

If intuition is something that you have a conscious desire to develop, acknowledging how you feel is where it all starts—which leads us to a discussion of the second definition: a quick and ready insight.

I have never experienced a complex thought process that was "quick." When I am trying to solve a problem in my head using thought, versus feeling, I am instantly aware of a distinct difference in the *knowing* that comes from trusting my intuition and the mental list that is running in my mind. I have also learned that when a strong feeling is direct opposition to a "logical" process I have created in my brain, and I side in favor of that logic, I am seldom pleased with the outcome.

Whether you already place a large amount of emphasis on intuition as a life skill or not, developing it by noticing what you feel about your decisions is going to serve you well. It will also replace the noise—and handicap—created by the voice of our ego.

Our ego's negative tapes that play over and over again can be quite powerful—like the one visiting me among these pages, constantly nagging "what makes you think you can write a book?"

I had dabbled in writing and crafted lyrics for songs, in addition to creating numerous press releases for my business and music promotions. My past experience seemed to indicate that my limited attention span for creating any work more than a few lines in length would be a huge barrier to doing a manuscript for a self-help book.

What made me realize that I should—and could—do this, was the way I *felt*. I was so on fire (pardon the pun) with the idea that I might have an experience that could help someone, that it felt uncomfortable *not* to be doing it. Had I thought seriously about the process, my lack of publishing knowledge, my need for an editor, the time and funds it would take to get it to press, the fact that I've never done this before, and the host of other items that "made sense" to me, I probably would have quit before I began!

Negative tapes are just that: negative and born out of ego, the part of our personality that tries to protect us. But ego will go a bit overboard if it is allowed to roam freely. Ego provides the "other" little voice that causes us to question our actions.

And because we are not in the habit of understanding that *feeling* provides us with a better direction, we often give into ego and let it sabotage the things we desire most of all.

The best illustration I can offer to help you understand the difference between the negative voice of ego and your intuition is illustrated by the book example. When

I'm writing, the gnawing desire to get these words on paper goes away. In following the voice of my intuition I have satisfied the requirement it had for me and it has nothing more to say. I feel relief. I feel good.

When I temporarily give in to my fear and decide I'm going to scrap the whole thing, *ego just keeps talking about it.* "See, I told you that you didn't have what it takes. Now look at what you've done. You went and got yourself all fired up for nothing. You wasted all that time and energy and what do you have to show for it? When are you going to learn to just stick with what you know? You should have learned by now…you will only be disappointed—believe me, it is much safer this way…"

*Once you start becoming aware of how you feel, following your intuition will always provide you some measure of relief or make you feel better when you act on it; ego on the other hand, keeps nagging—even after you have done everything it would ask of you.*

Your intuition will always be there to guide you to your next step if you can clear the noise long enough to feel it. Whether you are looking for that life-changing inspired purpose; trying to find the means to get there; or need to find a way out of your grief that represents some loss, take time to get quiet and ask: what is the next step? The answer may come in a way that will surprise you.

In my story, I share the experience of conversing with a monk in my meditation. As I mentioned, the exchange was not always a verbal conversation that I could recall later on. It was fairly common that I would receive a gift or item from the monk that I may or may not have recognized as a familiar shape or statue. My *feeling* around this was that the item would afford me some information when I had need for it or was ready to understand it better later on. When the time was right and I needed it most, I usually received some much-needed insight which felt like it was connected to the experience of receiving a gift.

Next time you find yourself feeling lost, try an experiment: *ask*. Asking is the first step, whether it is an inquiry to God, Christ, the Angels, your Higher Self or any thing or power that represents a greater intelligence. It's not about being religious; it is about being in touch with what you *feel* and giving those feelings the credibility they deserve. The next step then becomes acknowledging receipt of an answer.

**Trust that you received the answer and will be given the next step _whenever it is most appropriate for your highest good._**

If you are having trouble with this concept because it goes against what has been logical for you in the past, (and thereby a product of thought rather than feeling) I would respectfully point out that whether you know it or not, at some time you have acted on intuition already.

I give you exhibit A: reading this book.

When we make any choice to pick up something that is unknown, even a book, we can offer any number of reasons that led us to making that choice. The cover or title may have caught our attention, it may have been recommended by a friend, perhaps it was the only one available on the subject that we could easily find in the bookstore. Whatever reason we give, we still made a conscious decision to purchase something before we knew of the contents based on what we *felt* to be of benefit.

So I challenge you, once again, to feel those feelings and ask yourself: of all the books that were available...
...why did you pick this one?

# Sacred Fire Boarding Pass

PERMISSION · GRANTED · TO · COME · ABOARD

Notes
_____
Journal Entries

# Chapter Eleven

## One More Birthday

*"I would not exchange these few lines on my face*
*They are a word to the wise—a disregard for disgrace*
*A new decade's comin' that I'm gonna embrace*
*'Cause it's the dawning of a new age, now..."*
*...from* Dawn of a New Age, *song lyrics*
*- Adrianna Larkin -*

Imagine that you could have the same joy, excitement, anticipation, and expectancy of "something wonderful about to happen" that you used to have with your birthday when you were a kid. That is what sacred fire is all about, and it is what we can have again...if we are willing to consider another kind of birthday: one in which we are reborn into the life of *possibility*.

What if, as we grew older, our birthdays actually served as a marker of our youth, vitality, and passion—in addition to offering that childlike sense of expectancy and anticipation for the coming year? Birthdays would then once again take on a magical quality instead of marching us toward our mortality.

The only belief that stands between us and the feeling

I described above (which reclaims that magic) is a belief that we are somehow imperfect *and need something we don't have.*

About three weeks before turning 50 I was having a conversation with my son who was working in our shop at the time. In a dialogue that started with me "thinking out loud" I was reminded that I was in danger of doing exactly that: considering myself imperfect and lacking—all because of a number.

In what I thought was a very clever and insightful commentary, I explained my growing awareness of "rapid declining value due to a decreased ability to either be 'eye candy' or have babies—both of which are markers for feminine worth in western society."

He laughed—not out of insensitivity, but because he saw something else which I was about to understand myself as the bigger picture.

His unexpected insight was about to be revealed. "Granted, I don't know what it's like to be a 50-year old female. But this seems funny to me. Your songwriting is off the charts. You're composing better stuff than I can ever remember. Your voice has actually *improved* with age. You are creating—not your first—but your fourth CD that is actually due to go to press the day *before* your birthday—all in addition to running your own business. You have a great home, a great marriage, so what is it that you're lacking…"

And the final question that brought it all home was: "*What* do you want that you don't have?"

I just looked at him. His question had momentarily rendered me mute, admittedly a rare occurrence. He would take full advantage of this opportunity to make his point as he continued, however. "It may take seeing the CD finished, Mom…but I think by the time that happens your birthday will be just a footnote…"

Of course he was right, but here is what I got out of that conversation: The common factor linking my despair at turning 25 (that was the hard one) to what I believed to be gone at age 50 was a *perceived* loss of youth.

Loss which had not even registered on any of the 25 or so birthdays in between!

Note the emphasis on "perceived." This seems like the perfect time to bring up a concept that would later be titled as a song: *Perception is Nine-Tenths of the Law* – which means it's time to draft some new legislature.

We take on a monumental task in deciding to reform the "glass half empty" state. We have been conditioned to always need and always want with a definition of success furnished by mainstream media that is based upon the measurement of things acquired versus *who we really are*.

And the terribly distressing part of all this is that it is not routine advertising alone that is the culprit. If it were simply limited to needing whiter teeth, a lawn mower that trims your grass in half the time or a better tasting peanut butter, that would be one thing. But the sad truth is it has gone far beyond that. We are willing to throw everything – from divine gifts and experience, to our own good health and common sense – under the bus, just so we don't *perceive* that loss.

And that is why I emphasized *feeling* in the first chapter as a key to what is real, and what is valuable. If you choose to eliminate any other advice in the remainder of this book, it is my hope that getting in touch with the feeling of your own truth will be the one thing you take away with you when you close the back cover.

Even our so-called factual information has been contaminated to a large degree. Try to find a major U.S. news source that does not seem to favor one political party over another. The worst offenders, in my humble opinion, are the self-styled "political pundits."

These guys are the equivalent of Mickey Mouse as the sorcerer's apprentice. In the absence of intellect or any real skill to examine issues from a platform of impartial analysis, they use dark magic to cast their spell of fear. Like Mickey's broom in the classic cartoon, they look to this fear to do their work for them as they carelessly play, remaining cavalier and ignorant of the tremendous damage caused by the overflowing cauldron of public insecurity — even as it spills out of control. And all is excused by the networks as long as ratings are spilling over with everything else.

How could you know that you were impoverished / in danger / economically disadvantaged before they told you so? If you were feeling that way already, how much help were they in *relieving* that condition? (I have yet to see any of them offer their own resources...)

We must accept that we are in the perfect moment and needing nothing to reclaim our personal divinity which offers a legacy of well being. Then and only then can we take responsibility for our own reinvention.

And if we don't? We just reinforce the illusion that we are lacking something vital and allow our lives to be carefully manipulated by others for their own personal gain.

One of the most memorable roles I have seen played by Jim Carrey was that of the lead character in *The Truman Show*. This character goes about his life completely unaware in the beginning that his entire day-to-day existence was being broadcast to the rest of the country as a television program. His wife, boss, everyone he thought related to him, were actors who took long term roles so that the scam (and the program) could continue. At some point he starts to notice the pattern and trusts his instinct leading him to discover that everything he thought was "real" was a movie set and he has *always* had the power to break loose.

That is the rebirth I would like you to consider now — because that analogy offers more truth than you know.

Even if you are not yet prepared to accept that you are the creator of your life with unlimited potential, consider this: just on the outside chance, allowing for the smallest hint of possibility — however microscopic it may seem — that you can have all that you desire, that it is actually just outside the door of a movie set in that field of possibility, wouldn't you want to peek through the keyhole instead of dead-bolting the door to keep it out?

Did you laugh at the "deadbolt" description? Think it's ridiculous? The tragedy of our lives that gets repeated again and again is that we often do just that.

There is a common spiritual axiom that states: "What you want, wants you." I offer my own story as an example once again. How many times did I swear I was going to leave music behind "forever"? How many times was I coaxed back by something that I either considered as a "sign," wise counsel, or series of circumstances?

After what seemed like many "failed" attempts, it became *easier* to believe that I had missed out on what I needed as parental support. I was too burdened with responsibility. I didn't have the knowledge, the skill or the right circumstances to reinvent myself as a musician.

My reinvention — and a new kind of birthday — came with my declaration, supported by trust in the *possibility* that my music career could look completely different than I ever imagined and that I would be all right with that because it could be *better* than I had visualized. I now know, even though it bears little resemblance to what I imagined over two decades ago, it is *perfectly* aligned with what I want.

What if everything that *you* are now experiencing, feeling or thinking is perfect to bring you to your own pivotal moment of finding your personal sacred fire? You see, I believe that is exactly what has happened.

As children, before we knew ourselves to be limited, we would dream BIG. Because we could dream big, we could easily accept SMALL. A spoon or hair brush served as a microphone for me on more than one occasion. (It still can with more than one glass of wine, but that's another conversation.)

The point is that we didn't need everything *exactly* as we planned to become engaged. We were perfectly at peace having any part of the dream. Often accessing some part of the dream, like singing into a spoon, usually led to another part—like gathering an audience, which in turn led to people asking me to sing again, reinforcing a growing definition of being a singer...

Hopefully by now you get the idea: *you can cross the threshold at any time from any place.* And here's a little secret: doors are everywhere.

In our adult frame of mind, planning as we do for our lives, the lives of our children, the lives of aging parents or anything else—we forget:

**We don't need all the pieces to show up for our rebirth to occur; we just need <u>one</u> to serve as a point of entry.**

I recently had a conversation with a long-time friend who worked with me in the emergency room. During a really low point after the loss of a job, he called to say things seemed so bad he didn't know when he felt more removed from anything close to joy in his life. He couldn't see from his outlook *now* how he might ever feel good again. We talked very little about the job, but I did pose this question:

"If money were no object, and time had no limits, what would you do?"

"Go sailing," he said, just like that. His response was immediate — he did not even hesitate. But before I could ask him "why" he continued: "I *love* being on the water." He went on to say how this gave him a sense of freedom and release as he described all the physical sensations of the wind in his face and the warmth of the sun, or the slight chill that made him alive in the absence of any sun at all. The more he spoke about it the more his tone changed, and it would easily seem that within a five-minute window he had accomplished what we think only pharmaceuticals can: he had elevated his mood sufficiently to gain an entry to his own rebirth.

"There's your answer," I replied. It was a statement that, by itself, over-simplified the issue. The over-simplification was further compounded by the fact that he lives in a landlocked Midwestern locale.

"I don't know *how*..." he began.

Or where...or when... But as we talked, I told him of my own experience at a lake resort that had a yacht club. I explained that it had been an accidental discovery, as it was one of the best kept secrets in my part of west/central Illinois. Just a few miles from cornfields and barns, I had located this lake that was gaining increased popularity in the summer. While reviewing the activities offered, I noticed that the yacht club offered a "guest day" to share the joy of sailing with the local community. (It also served as a recruiting day to enlist deck hands for some of the racing activities that originated from there.)

The conversation grew long, and my friend

mentioned a few people he knew who were avid boaters and even owned sailboats. When I asked him, he agreed they might be willing to teach/barter/even share with him if he expressed an interest...

Voicing that interest was the door that he opened. When I last spoke with him he had already crossed the threshold to share the experience of sailing with a friend who was more than delighted to share *his* vessel and love of the water with someone who demonstrated the same passion for boating.

It's like I said: what you want, wants you....

When we think of rebirth, we often think we should jump from the opening credits to the very end of the movie. However, if we did that, what would be lost in the unfolding of our story? Even for those we consider to be privileged, successful, or the perfect example of what we wanted to be when we grew up, we seldom see what lay behind the scenes for them to get there.

Even though I heard tales of many successful musicians who were the "20-year overnight success" stories, I thought my own story should be different. The truth is our arrival at the full blown culmination of our purpose may take the form of a gentle unfolding. But whether "quick" by your own definition or the culmination of years to connect:

**It is as perfect for you as you are for the experience.**

All you have to remember to do is to leave the door open.

I don't claim to know what happens when we leave

this earth plane for an existence outside of our physical bodies. I have stretched my own beliefs to think that I have been physical many times in the past and will choose to become physical again. That creates an even greater sense of urgency that I can't wait for another life to arrive at what I desire for this one. The opportunity may never come again.

Even if you believe we live only in this existence and spend eternity as souls, it is certainly tragic to think that we would not make the most of it.

And so for believers of reincarnation and nonbelievers alike, I offer a challenge: Know that *within you* lies the power to be reborn *in this lifetime* with all that you need and the perfect set of circumstances – just by considering the *possibility* of everything you're going through right now as being part of the plan.

Then I would ask the question: If money were no object and time had no limits *with anything at all being possible*, what would you most like to do?

Write it down: _____

_____

_____

_____

_____

_____

If you are still having trouble bringing this into focus, try something else. What keeps showing up as a recurring theme in your life right now?

_____

_____

_____

_____

_____
_____

What do you feel that you have talents for already? __

_____
_____
_____
_____
_____
_____

This one might be more difficult—but If you would seek to go from where you are to where you want to be, how might this happen, almost as if "by magic"? _____

_____
_____
_____
_____
_____
_____

What steps can you take to make it more likely for that magic to happen? _____

_____
_____
_____
_____
_____
_____

Take a good look at your answers, think about them, imagine the possibilities and change them or add to them as inspiration strikes. There are no rules for our rebirth—only the choice of which doorway we choose to walk through. All we have to do is turn the handle and leave the door ajar just a bit to let in the light of possibility. The threshold that gets crossed when we're ready will always be the one that is best matched to our desires.

So go ahead, live it up! Dream and think BIG…make a new wish or dust off an old one. It's *your* birthday.

# Sacred Fire Boarding Pass

PERMISSION · GRANTED · TO · COME · ABOARD

Notes

Journal Entries

# Chapter Twelve

### Pick Up the Remote

*"Something enchanted became familiar,*
*your presence a melody sung in my dream,*
*Although I had tried a whole lifetime to write this*
*its rhythm was always elusive..."*
*...from* Friends and Lovers, *song lyrics*
- Adrianna Larkin -

I had the pleasure of interviewing Dr. Bruce Lipton, author of *The Biology of Belief* (Mountain of Love / Elite Books, 2005) on my radio program. I had always tried to keep an open mind regarding the heredity versus environment argument, but after an hour-long conversation with Dr. Lipton, environment gained a lot more ground.

He made a compelling case as he shared his findings that adopted children acquired the same type of cancer that runs in certain families — even rare forms of cancers — with the same frequency as blood relatives. If we can make a case for our programming and environment in the creation of a "random" disease, what else can that same conditioning create?

I believe our programming starts before birth, as we now know that sounds are heard by a fetus in the womb. Before we even have mastery of our language we are guided and "formed" from the expressions, gestures, vocal volume, and feelings as they are communicated by our caregivers. We receive messages that include *judgments* about everything in our world, and those judgments become the beliefs that create the world as we know it.

Here's the point that we want to remember however: those who helped shape our beliefs — parents, siblings, teachers, and friends — were programmed in the same way! They received judgments that were passed onto them, in addition to forming some new ones based on *their* personal experience.

What that means for us then is before we can walk, talk or have free reign to collect our own experiences, we have been given a select group of channels and our "viewing habits" have already been decided for us.

Hence, what we think we "know" then has been largely dictated by a set of beliefs that is not even relevant — *except through perception* – to any experience of our own!

I will challenge you to consider the possibility — however improbable — that nothing you think you know currently exists. You can point to physical laws that surround "real" things like matter and light; but as the best and brightest scientific minds are discovering, there is room to question what we once thought was absolute in these areas as well. So that begs another question: in the world as it is today, what *is* real, finite, and unshakeable, as a single truth we can rely on?

The answer: *Whatever we choose to <u>believe</u>.*

In the most basic-sense definition, I've heard it said that a belief is *just a thought* that we rethink again and again. That being said, we all have certain beliefs that no longer serve us. These are the reruns we've seen a hundred times, and so very often they are the few episodes we didn't even like — even if we were once big fans of the show. Let's swap these worn out programs for some new ones.

In order to do that, we have to look at all the ways we feel ourselves to be challenged. These are usually "spinoffs" of our earliest programs. They show up as lack of skill, a character flaw, circumstances, time, age, gender, ethnicity, religion, education or anything that you *believe* to be a barrier.

Our ability to change channels lies in the understanding that nothing is "real" as we know it. Our "reality" is only what we *believe,* <u>and we can change those beliefs</u>!

Are you ready to use the remote?

When it came time to record the title track to *Sacred Fire*, I stumbled across an unexpected "rerun" of my own. I decided I wanted a flute part to accent the song and really lend the feel of something primal. I could hear the part in my head, hear and *feel* how it should be played. I only needed one thing more: someone to play it.

Those I had tried to reach were not available in the time frame I needed it done. It seemed the only answer left to me was to take out my own flute that had remained essentially untouched for 30 years. Oddly enough, I had total recall of the fingering placement for each note. I did have to practice to reacquire the muscle tone to produce the clarity, but after a few weeks I was able to gain that also.

And as I practiced, as I played, and as I improved, I began to time travel in my thoughts. I had always liked playing flute—what had changed that?

I had started my flute studies in the 6th grade, two years later than everyone else. My instructor was a delightful man who loved kids and loved music, and more than anything delighted in the alchemy of bringing the two together. In this mix I had thrived and found myself holding first chair. I no doubt had an advantage in that my experience with the piano-teaching aunt had taught me to read music and apply memory for combinations that seemed easily transferable from piano to flute. But most of all I loved the sound I could make with it.

At the end of the year when summer band was set to start, my instructor arranged for me to play with a high school group. I was thrilled that someone believed in me so much. He explained how this challenge at two years above my grade level would hone my performance and take me to the next level. He recommended to Mom that I study at the conservatory near our home for advanced instruction in the fall.

I finished that summer to begin training at the conservatory where I had a much different encounter. I was assigned to a young man who was, in my very self-conscious and sensitive 12-year old experience, just plain *mean*. Before I even opened my flute case it seemed I could feel his contempt. He didn't want any part of someone else's idea of a prodigy. I couldn't stand right, breathe right, turn the page right—let alone perform with any skill. It seemed at times that the mere idea of me even showing up was cause for criticism and it was made quite apparent that I lacked any skill...

At least that is what I *believed*.

All of this came flooding back to me. I now understand it simply as my first encounter with an unpleasant experience in anything related to the performance of music. It shook my very core though, but mainly because *I had not come to terms with it until 30 years later*.

Imagine my response then when I realized I was replaying the same tired rerun of a badly written episode. One whose only claim to fame was its ability to make me feel 12 years old again as I held *any* instrument in my hand...

How much better would I have been served if I considered the possibility, (however *remote)* that the episode was just one I didn't like and I could exchange it for another?

After years of seeking knowledge and studying metaphysical properties of energy, it all gets back to what I remember as a high school science lesson beautifully described as the Law of Conservation of Energy: "Energy is neither created nor destroyed."

We *can* absolutely transform it, however — and as you can probably see from my own example, our limiting beliefs carry a *lot* of energy.

Especially those beliefs related to our worthiness. The "right" to live the life of our dreams, one filled with passion, purpose, and prosperity, poses the greatest challenge because it is tied to beliefs that come from our earliest programming and therefore are easily overlooked. They take many forms, but most commonly resemble some version of the following (and all ones that I have used myself):

- "What makes you think you can do this?" (not skilled/smart/strong enough)
- "My family won't approve." (my own happiness is not important)
- "Nobody would want my product." (I offer nothing of value)
- "Other people are lucky, not me." (I don't deserve to win)
- "That ship has already sailed." (My dreams have an expiration date)

***Anytime you <u>diminish your own desire</u> rather than seek support for it, you are dealing with an aspect of being unworthy.***

In the last chapter, I did my best to make a case for the jumping off point of reinvention being exactly where you are at that point in time. That is not to say that once we cross the threshold that our work is done. Intent is a necessary part of the equation, but *inspired action* is necessary for completion of that intent.

Inspired action helps to transform the energy so that we can change the program to something useful that serves our needs from that which does not...bringing to mind a tiny framed print I received from a friend more than a decade ago and one I still keep displayed. Like so many simplistically profound moments, the words were attributed to the most prolific writer of all time: Anonymous. But doing real-time research, I discovered that I can thank Carl Bard for the words: "No one can go back and make a brand new start, but anyone can start from now and make a brand new ending."

Using the example of my flute and its thirty-year hibernation, I remembered from my earlier experience that it took some practice to get the clarity of tone. The same tone I wanted for recording — so *practice* was the missing link. I felt *inspired* to take the time to do it so that my intention could be completed, and in doing so...

I rewrote my whole program.

If you have ever completed a short term goal, such as running a marathon, applying for a job, or learning to belly dance, didn't you train, prepare or practice? We really can use any place as our point of entry, but once we cross that threshold, we accomplish little if remain near the safety of the door. The idea is to move forward with action appropriate for our final outcome.

And just because you have identified the missing pieces needed to form the picture and have gained some comfortable forward momentum, don't think that the voice of ego will stay silent. Too often it seems that just when you are closest to settling in with a bowl of popcorn to enjoy a new show, ego can become the most rambunctious — and the most self-sabotaging — by replaying old beliefs. This little guy means well, he just doesn't believe there could be anything better than those old reruns!

When we talked about inspired action following intent, there was a reason for the word "inspired": it *supports* the intent. Many times our ego likes to lead us to the land of "should" — just to keep us from changing the channel. Any statement surrounding an action that begins with "I should" needs to be closely examined. "Should" tends to be born out of *obligation*, not *inspiration*. Things like:

- I should take better care of myself
- I should keep a better house
- I should take more overtime at work

...are all creatures of obligation, but why don't we examine them in light of support for our intent to see if they lend equal support to our inspiration:

**"I should take better care of myself."** If your intent is to own your own business within a year, taking care of yourself actually supports that intent. How successful do you think you will be if you have even minor health issues that you are refusing to address? The role played by your well-being in the success of acquiring and maintaining a business is significant. Inspired action might be monitoring how you feel and making necessary changes to support good health for your own peak performance.

**"I should keep a better house."** As one who regularly preached to my offspring the tenets of good hygiene and sane living, one might be inclined to think I could pass a white glove inspection. Not quite. I do what is necessary to meet basic needs, but frankly there is frequently more dust than shine on furnishings (unless we are expecting company — then the cursory wipe down is given) and I have become fine with that because with time being limited, I can best support my goal of performance by attending auditions, preparing marketing, accepting gigs, and seeking other work when necessary to supplement my income, *instead* of obsessing over my housekeeping skills.

**"I should take more overtime at work."** This is entirely dependent on how it supports your intent. Do you

124

require extra income to launch your dream of buying a business or do you require more time to research an area or gain skills for running the business? Is the desire for income only based on satisfying some guilt you have for the pursuit of your dream or will it furnish a nest egg to tie you over while the business is growing?

By examining every action in light of what support is offered for our intent, we can get to "inspiration point" which offers more fuel to grow the sacred fire, *as we enjoy our new programs.*

Then at least when you hear the voice of ego telling you to do something, you will recognize it for what it is. And if that voice continues to challenge your worthiness (as mine so often does) you can try this. It's a little visual exercise I created that may be of help.

When that voice of doubt shows up to make some noise, try pretending that the voice is a small child who is overtired and acting out; at which point you can pick it up, take it to bed, tuck it in, and after reminding it that everything is okay in the world you both share, kiss it goodnight.

What are the words you could offer that child if he/she appeared right now? _____

_____

_____

_____

_____

_____

_____

The goal isn't to silence the voice completely — it has a role to fill in keeping us safe and protected in addition to creating positive aspects of our personality. But it is important that you start to become better able to tell the difference between what serves your true purpose and what is a leftover from a limiting belief system — *especially* if it is from a past experience attached to your self worth.

As our twenty-first century resources give us amazing opportunities and tools to reinvent ourselves, they can offer really unique hiding places to keep us replaying the old reruns. Overextended and short on sleep, buried in paperwork and too many things to do, we can lose ourselves in a whirlwind of activity that never links to our intent and keeps us too far removed from our feelings as we watch the same tired shows.

There is an old expression that says "nothing changes unless you do." If you are on the constant go from one project to another, one meeting to another, one event to another, there is little room for any time to imagine what you would like to be different and what might be standing in the way.

So let's take some time now.

What do you feel might be limiting you at this time?

_____

_____

_____

_____

_____

_____

_____

_____

How could this be related to a worn out belief system? _____

_____
_____
_____
_____
_____
_____
_____

What belief could be substituted for one that no longer serves, such as "I'm too old to start a music career" as being exchanged for "I'm at the perfect place in life to start a music career?"

_____
_____
_____
_____
_____
_____
_____
_____

List the supporting reasons for your intent, such as "my children are grown and out of college, so I have less responsibility/more time for music." _____

_____
_____
_____
_____
_____
_____

_____
_____
_____

What actions can support your intent? (i.e. research of places that hire musicians) _____

_____
_____
_____
_____
_____
_____
_____
_____

What actions work against that intent? _____

_____
_____
_____
_____
_____
_____
_____
_____

This is your chance to pick up what "remote-ly" serves you and keep channel surfing until you find a show you really like...one that fits...one with clever, intelligent writers who have scripted the perfect ending for _you_. It deserves "prime time" with inspired action.

Because anything less is just another rerun.

# Chapter Thirteen

## Truth and Dare

*"Taking chances, so you can play the game and then you dance in
Like a moth around a flame, but danger enhances,
this drive you cannot tame, because you release the hounds to start the chase
If you're not living life on the edge, you're taking up too much space..."*
...from Life on the Edge, *song lyrics*
- Adrianna Larkin -

We can use many labels to define the same thing: *Heart's Desire, Inspired Purpose, Actualization, Right Livelihood.* Call it what you will, but it is important to understand that there is a dramatic difference between reinventing yourself to one of these descriptions and the pursuit of a new career. One is the light of our divinity; the other is the safe zone. Or more simply: one is your truth—the other is a substitute for that truth.

And only one is fueled by sacred fire.

Sacred fire is basically a metaphor for what drives us to live with clear intention. It is the spark of divinity that defines what we came here to do—the light that leads many to what we can more easily describe as destiny. I believe it is what we came here to do in *this* lifetime. You may know it as simply what makes you feel good. Having the ability to embrace it fully will create the excitement for the start of each new day.

*Sacred fire fuels the richness and personal fulfillment that joins with a sense of purpose not found in other activities.*

It is the "juice" for that thing which presents as a unique talent or gift—a gift which offers benefit to others both directly and indirectly. That benefit may not even be seen (at least initially) by the person who offers it. When natural ability is present, self-perception often labels it as "nothing special" or "just something I like to do."

In acting on our purpose, sacred fire has a way of meeting our monetary needs, or leading us to other sources that meet those needs. Whatever it gives back takes the form of real personal wealth that has the potential to leave us satisfied far above what we thought possible before embracing it—and more than what money *without* that passion could bring. When aligned with it, we find that we are seldom without what we really need.

*The secret to reaping the wealth of sacred fire is not to do battle with it.*

As odd as this seems, doing battle with it is often precisely what happens. Sacred fire has so much pull, and its desire to point us toward our own truth can seem so strong, that oftentimes running away from it or fighting with it is exactly what we do to remain in the illusion and away from our truth...in a self-defeating game of hide and seek. We mask it with descriptions of "irresponsible" or "unimportant" and exchange it for the comfort of what we know: the programming of our environment.

Sacred fire has the ability to show us the essence of who we really are, but only if we are willing to take off the blinders. We all know what makes us feel good. We all know what we enjoy, what we would seek to do again and again. Likewise we know what doesn't feel good and what we don't like to do. At the risk of sounding like a broken record: our feelings are the key—and usually what we liked doing as a child offers many clues to our purpose as we grow older.

**More Than One Right Answer** ~ What if you like to do many different things? What if you cannot connect a greater purpose to what you do at all? What if you were doing something you really loved but circumstances changed, and now it feels like you are forced to do something else? These are all questions that we will ask and answer in this chapter.

**The Enjoyment of Many Things** ~ My friend Lynn Scheurell, who playfully refers to herself as "The Guru of Woo-Woo" ([www.mycreativecatalyst.com](www.mycreativecatalyst.com)), is a talented business intuitive who counsels entrepreneurs and individuals who are, in her words, "renaissance people." Her clients have a variety of talents and interests—along with a number of skills to support them—and they often seek Lynn's help to funnel down to what they will obtain the *most* satisfaction and fulfillment from.

Choice is a great thing. But too many choices can be overwhelming. When you feel pulled in a variety of areas it is a good idea to get input from those who support you and have your best interest at heart. Ask for their feedback of what they see as your strengths, your greatest satisfaction, those things you do with *ease*. Make a list, then *see what feels like "truth" to you.*

Notice that I said "support you" — there should be a clear distinction made between those who wish to see you reach your dreams and the "dream stealers" that often come in the form of negative friends, family, coworkers or anyone else who may be threatened by your growth. Sonia Choquette, (www.soniachoquette.com) author of *Your Heart's Desire: Instructions for Creating the Life You Really Want* (Three Rivers Press, 1997) was a guest on my radio program. She offers a beautiful phrase to describe that support offered from those who know you. She recommends that you use their "believing eyes" to help shore up your desires and overcome doubt.

Many times "too many choices" are just that: the product of too much self-doubt, too much over-thinking. There is a familiar and recurring pattern for many of us, starting things and then finding it difficult to complete those tasks before moving on to something else. Having wrestled with this myself, I think there are larger forces at play than just a lack of discipline.

As we move through the completion of any project, especially one that is new to us, it's to be expected that we will come up against things that create a temporary road block. It is during these times of challenge that multi-talented individuals will turn to something else that they know how to do very well to get the satisfaction of remaining in their comfort zone. But what if we took the time to get past whatever is holding us up?

Something I call the "Quitters Bargain" is a little game that can be played between you and yourself to help do just that—and yes, the opposing you-s can be adversaries. But they can also, happily or begrudgingly, join forces to navigate the detours. So the next time you feel you have lost the initial excitement for a project and decide to move on to something else, stop and ask: what is the barrier to finishing this? If it is another tool, a resource, more knowledge or anything you can identify as a possible means of addressing the problem, consult with the people who have those "believing eyes", as Sonia says, or do your own research to find out how it might be fixed.

Whatever your tactic, strike a bargain with yourself that you will only "quit" after you have gotten past the barrier and things are going smoothly again. In fact, try to adopt the mindset that you can move on to that other thing that is waiting for you and make *that* the goal of completing this one. It's funny how well this works. Not to mention that you will also develop some great problem-solving skills that will transfer over to everything else.

**Connecting to Great Purpose** ~ My friend Barb waited years to buy her own home. In a series of events that were the byproduct of her corporate life, business investments, things that made owning property a burden, she delayed home ownership as a conscious choice. Now in her 40s, she has purchased her first home *and thoroughly enjoys it*. So much so that many weekends are dedicated to working on it to the exclusion of many social activities. Is this great purpose?

I believe it is...*if* it is born out of joy. I tend to think that a few years from now, Barb will be so skilled at basic elements of carpentry and home repair that she will be able to teach it. Joy is expansive. We can't help but learn and grow with it. We can't contain it—even if we try—and will find ways to share it that we may never understand completely.

The day I went with Barb to pick out her patio furniture, we arrived at a situation that could be likened to fitting a room full of furnishings into a clown car. It was actually a minivan and five not-so-easy preassembled pieces, but it yielded the same result. Laughing outrageously in our own determination to solve the puzzle and successfully transport everything home in one trip, we could barely get it done. But we have fully embraced the experience as one of humor and history as we continue to reminisce and re-live the gorgeous sunset, great breeze, and celebratory glass of wine we enjoyed once the furniture was safely home, unloaded, and in place. Her humor, peace, joy, and excitement were the gifts she shared with me in creating the experience of nesting in her own space.

Whether it is spending time with your children—which greatly enriches their lives if done so joyously—working in your garden, scrap-booking to retain memories for future generations, restoring a classic car, I believe:

*Any activity performed in a state of joy contributes to the wealth of the world, in addition to offering unlimited potential to reveal itself as an important piece of your destiny.*

**Having to Surrender What You Love** ~ This is the hardest one of all. Especially if that "something" was a primary means of employment or a long-term relationship. Understand that the human tendency is to color even the best events of the past with rose colored glasses. When something that we had an emotional connection to is suddenly removed from our day to day reality, it is normal to feel that sense of loss.

But *feeling* is exactly what we need to do. At times the sense of loss is so devastating that we would do anything to get out from under it. And because of that we may take on any number of tactics from overburdening ourselves with activity to overeating or substance abuse to keep from feeling anything at all.

If you can get to the point of allowing yourself that sense of sadness, even if it seems overwhelming at times, it can actually afford a wonderful opportunity to decide how much of what you are feeling is a sense of loss versus fear of moving forward.

In my observation, some people who complain the loudest about the loss of their jobs are the same ones who were the most vocal about the fact they did not like it. Still, the security of having that job meant they did not have to look for anything else. Security...the word itself is often voiced in reverent tones. But it has a dark side—one that often serves as an oppressive anchor that keeps us weighed in at the fear end of what we described earlier as the Love/Fear continuum.

Oftentimes things "go away" for something better. That includes relationships. What looms large for us in the space that was vacated by a person is the *possibility* of it becoming perfect even if it was less than perfect before. This is never more pronounced than when you are not the one who ended the relationship.

My husband Mike, who was married 18 years before he met me, can easily recall the devastation he felt when his first wife expressed a desire to start over without him. He really didn't think he would find anyone he would be compatible with again. And as my story clearly indicates in the beginning of this book, neither did I. We each had our own version of an empty space. But thankfully, with time, we were able to fill that space with another possibility.

Which brings us the next leg of our journey: it is at this time I would like to extend an invitation. You are cordially invited to join me in accessing unlimited potential for personal bliss. The attire is casual, there is nothing to bring. All I ask is the honor of your presence on that same field of possibility. The possibility you visited so many times for that relationship, that job, experience, or whatever was plucked from your grasp that you fought so hard to hold onto. It is the same place you can go to again to quell the fear of the unknown. The beauty of it is: *all you have to do is show up.*

And as I mentioned earlier, you've been here before.

"Masterminding" is one of my favorite vehicles for transport to the field of possibility. Whether used to find your purpose, overcoming the roadblocks or simply complete a project, it offers a great tool for accessing our unlimited potential with the help of those "believing eyes."

I began to understand the value masterminding could have for me when a friend introduced me to the work of Mary Robinson Reynolds (www.makeadifference.com). I had read Napoleon Hills' reference to masterminding in his book *Think and Grow Rich.* (There are several reprints of this book, but I own the 1937 version published and distributed by www.AsAManThinkith.com.) While this book was my first introduction to the concept, Mary's website offered a wealth of information, a list of available courses, and a script accessible through a link on her site entitled *7 Steps to the Mastermind Connection.*

In the weekly mastermind group that I continue to use there are essentially two key parts. We begin by each person sharing what they felt were successes for the week. With the first declaration of success, the others in the group take a turn validating and congratulating the successes. Then comes a declaration of what that person would like to accomplish. The individuals in the group again take a turn, offering either a key connection, resource, or their own "believing eyes" to encourage and support. When one person finishes, someone else starts and the process begins again.

In a group created to support our fledgling radio network, we met weekly to take turns doing exactly this. The beauty of it is that the successes don't have to be huge; it might be something as simple as "I had switchboard problems last week, but managed to have a great show anyway—I call that a success."

I still mastermind with another host on a weekly basis and the focus has moved from the show to personal and spiritual growth. This simple exercise has kept me close to my own truth and it offered the support that "dared" me to live it. Although our group started with 5 members, it has downsized to just two, yet the growth for both of us has been remarkable and far reaching. The secret is to include members, (even if it is only one) who are *positive*. When we look for our "believing eyes" to come from people who are insecure in themselves, cannot—or refuse to—see another's strength, it is worse than no masterminding at all.

The ability to see that truth then--what really lies at the core of "who we are" — is the source of ignition for our personal sacred fire. We just have to be daring enough to embrace it.

In all of my former occupations — that of emergency room nurse, to corporate management, to owning my own business — nothing gave me the sense of wholeness or completeness I had after I declared my intention to become a full-time performer.

I was not prepared that this would lead me back in any way to my first love of acting either, but that is often the nice surprise that comes with the experience. It takes you to places you would never have considered in playing it safe, as it steers you away from many places whose hazards would remain hidden in what you may consider to be a refuge.

As I write this, I understand that it was my own sacred fire that directed me to business ownership. Upon receiving all that I needed from that experience, it set the stage for the close of that business, the filing of bankruptcy and preparation for foreclosure. It has at the same time offered the resources to know my own strength and ability to recover from these things. It reminded me of the joy that is found in family and the love of close friends, as it provided the backdrop for a closeness with my husband that I could not imagine experiencing without it.

Had I made another kind of decision — one much less daring — to forego a business purchase, I would have remained in corporate America. With my continued match on my 401K, there is a good degree of certainty (based on conversations I still have with those I worked with) that I would be working yet more hours at a job that had increasingly unrealistic demands with shrinking benefits and equally shrinking satisfaction.

I would have an hour commute and a 401K that would be less than half of what it was when I started at my last position. I would have most likely faced one, if not two, occurrences of downsizing—possibly at the same time as my husband. It is entirely feasible that, considering the job market for the 50-something age range, we would be attempting to live off of the shrinking 401K in an ever-competitive job arena and still be faced with the same situation of bankruptcy or foreclosure.

I would also have passed on the destination I have arrived at today: a remarkably peaceful place with the most incredible sense of joy I have known in my adult life.

So…it is with all this in mind that I challenge you to seek your truth. And remind you that the decisions we regret most often are not the indulgences we allowed…

…but the ones we did not dare to take.

# Sacred Fire Boarding Pass

PERMISSION · GRANTED · TO · COME · ABOARD

Notes
_____
Journal Entries

# Chapter Fourteen

## No Rules ~ Just Tools

*"As a kid I heard it said what you hold in your hand*
*is only what you can own,*
*There's one thing I've come to understand, now that I'm fully grown*
*It makes no difference what you say, if I know what I saw*
*Possession doesn't mean that much to me*
*It's my perception that's nine-tenths of the law."*
*...from* Perception, *song lyrics*
*- Adrianna Larkin -*

In the last chapter, we mentioned that you don't have to make your passion into your livelihood, but if you are going to work at something, why not something you *love*. The question then is how do we do that and not have it become a labor or take years to get there?

While there is nothing wrong with taking the scenic route (my own story indicates that I did just that) reinvention doesn't have to be as fickle as it was for me in the beginning. Just know that if you feel the uncertainty that accompanies a new venture, the reason may be as much physical as psychological.

In the movie *What the Bleep Do We Know!?*, (www.whatthebleep.com) there is an entertaining account of how established pathways in the brain support much of our behavior. With animated characters providing a neat little biology lesson, the movie does a good job of showing how we have to physically change and grow new pathways in the brain for new patterns of behavior to seem comfortable. It also talks about the receptors that support our emotional cravings, whether that craving is for food or drama or self doubt.

So the two key things to remember are:

1. You will frequently be out of your comfort zone with any activity that is not part of your current program.
2. There is a physical reason for that discomfort and it is <u>temporary</u> — *as long as you continue to challenge the discomfort with repetition.*

In short, all newness will seem strange for awhile as our brain remains "under construction." It takes about 21 days to form new habits or break old ones, largely due to the need for our bodies to create new cells and tissue that will support the change with what we know as comfort.

That applies to courage also.

The courage needed to reinvent ourselves and live our inspired purpose is usually not flawless. Seldom does it descend on us all at once with a great "aha!" moment. It is rarely the threshold that we cross that is seen as the point of no return. We cross it, we go back...we cross it again then retreat to the safety of the doorway. (Remember defeat, surrender, return?) Eventually, if we continue, we begin to remain on the side of bravery with longer intervals between the retreat and forward movement—as we seek shorter episodes of sanctuary.

So if it is true that courage is not the absence of fear but the ability to move forward in the face of it, and our physiology has to change to support the continued act of courage, then the first bold step is all that is really needed. The beauty that emanates from taking that first bold step is that it tends to make the next bold step a little easier, and the one after that easier still.

Challenging convention, your programming, your childhood traumas or whatever you have identified as your most common reason for "playing it safe" can be daunting, but it also leads to what I like to call the *root of reality*, otherwise known as:

"Who made that rule?"

In the case of "not having what it takes" or "not being able to earn a living at what you want"...*who made that rule*? If you dream about leaving your factory job to become an artist but are convinced you can't, go to your root of reality. In what stone tablet, ancient scroll or bathroom stall was it inscribed for the rest of us to see that you cannot have what you want. (As I ask this, a few of you will actually try to think of places where you might have seen it.) It doesn't matter if you think you can come up with one or not, the important question is to ask yourself: *who* made that rule?

For me the rule was made by my Dad who said so many times, "You can't be an actress, you'll starve"—which also carried over to a career in music by the way, as I found new and creative ways to not be paid for my work. Busting loose from this illusion to get at the root of my own reality I can come up with any number of people who are successful actors and performers and show every indication of being very well nourished.

And if you are still someone who needs permission to move forward, consider the ever-changing world that we live in that now makes it not only easier, but more common, to change careers, seek fulfillment, and reinvent ourselves.

The truth is that even though we may think some things are written in stone, we can find every kind of example from religious practice to laws of physics that say our reality is meant to change. Often these are modified as required by modern times, new research, better choices or greater insights.

My husband tells the story of growing up as one of seven children in a good Catholic family that always had fish on Friday. The church changed its position on requiring Catholics to consume fish on Friday while he still lived at home. His mom however, did not—and to this day still observes this once popular dictum. Not because she is short on faith, but because she is more comfortable doing what has always been done. This is her root of reality. But it also means that this is *her* rule and not that of the church.

No one had ever thought that anyone could beat the four-minute mile until Roger Bannister shattered that reality in 1954. Once it had been achieved, any number of athletes followed to run a mile in under four minutes and the "record" has been broken again and again.

The laws of physics that we now take for granted as supporting air travel were once believed impossible. Previously failed attempts and loss of life made any possibility of practical air travel seem like just another fantasy until the Wright brothers brought forth another set of rules.

A case begs to be made that someone must always be the first and that there is just one root of reality that we share universally:

***When it comes to reinventing your life, there are no rules except those you choose to experience for your own comfort.***

Once we realize this, *we no longer need permission.* That is not to say that we don't need to communicate with a partner or family members who may be impacted by our decision, but we don't need permission to "break the rules" *because there **are** none.*

**Two Practices** ~ Two tools (not rules) that will help you remain on the other side of the door for longer periods of time are:

1. Singularity of purpose
2. Alternate pathways

Both of these things are what I lacked in the early days of my career in music. Both have the power to work miracles and rework the odds that may seem like they are against you for any kind of successful reinvention.

**#1. Singularity of purpose** ~ This is what sacred fire brings to the table. It is the passion, the laser beam focus of what you want to do and what you like. It includes the delegation of the other aspects that you don't like as much, so you can completely focus on that which you can be good at and enjoy doing.

Now that music has become the focus, I have turned over the promotions and logistics of planning to my husband who enjoys doing this—and that allows me to be free to create, perform, and attend auditions. Although there always seem to be elements of our inspired purpose that are not as engaging to us as others, the less favorable parts should not be a barrier to seeking that experience.

And if you continue to have any protracted fear, doubt, insecurity, ambiguity or conflict as to your ability or worthiness to work in your passion, then the reinvention process becomes much more difficult. It is not impossible, but it can be difficult.

If you find yourself torn between an obligation to others and your heart's desire, you may wish to wait to go "full throttle" before you take that leap of faith. It is fine to make the decision to defer a full-time pursuit of your ideal career if you are still in the stages of raising children or caring for an aging parent. If your are torn between duty to those dependent upon you, then the conflict that is created only works against singularity of purpose and you won't be able to support your own success as effectively as if you did not have the conflict.

**#2. Alternate pathways** ~ As much as we would like to own a crystal ball at times, it is much better that we don't. If you have found the means to be active with something you love to do, *enjoy* it. Do as much of it as humanly possible and unburden yourself from the belief that it has to turn out a certain way. It may in fact lead you to something else you like equally well or another aspect you may even like *more*.

It's absolutely wonderful if what you enjoy doing

most can be made into a career—but if you are honestly convinced that it can't, that doesn't mean you should value it any less. It may, in fact, start as a hobby, a pastime or a temporary position that takes you to something else and *evolves* to a career later on. You will never know unless you are taking every opportunity to indulge in it.

At one time, I believed the only way I could have a career in music was to craft songs for commercial release. The fact is that I really didn't like the pitch sessions and submissions which took up most of my time, and what I liked most was writing, followed by recording and performing my own material. (Yes, even with my lack of confidence, performance was still more enjoyable than the business mechanics of trying to get a song published.) And that brings us back to singularity of purpose.

In short: our purpose should be defined, but not the pathway to get there. To help clearly define the purpose and leave the pathway open, I offer the *list of ten*. These are qualities and attributes that I initially compiled as a guidepost for a mate. Upon the advice of a friend who knew a good deal more about relationships than I did, I used his process to hone in on qualities I wanted in a partner. But I have since used the *list of ten* for things beyond the romantic caliber. It works very well for careers—which, if you think about it, is just another mode of partnership.

In the *list of ten* there is only one guidepost (again no rules, just tools): For the desired result—be it a mate or a career—nothing less than 90% is acceptable. Generally speaking, if 90% of the attributes are not present, the satisfaction will not be either.

This really forces you to carve out what is most important to you in a relationship of any kind: either with another person or your livelihood. For a frame of reference, I am sharing the list I created before meeting Mike and the one I have since crafted for my career. It can also be a tool to decide what you would like in a house, a school, or anything else that you wish to acquire.

My *list of ten* for my perfect partner (Mike had all ten):

1. Strong work ethic
2. Open-minded
3. Excellent communication skills
4. Non-smoker
5. Healthy/works out
6. Values family
7. Good money manager
8. Affectionate
9. Spontaneous
10. Dependable

My *list of ten* for a perfect career:

1. Autonomy
2. Extreme creativity
3. Receive credit for products I create
4. Variable work schedule
5. Potential for pay greater than three times my highest salary
6. Allows my mate to be involved
7. Offers benefit to humanity
8. Interpersonal interaction (as opposed to isolated work)
9. Products created that remain after I am gone
10. Not confined to one location

Notice that I picked *qualities* of that career rather than naming the actual career itself. This leaves room for it to appear different than I may have imagined, yet still contain all of the elements I desire. I tend to think my "perfect" career will be music, perhaps something yet related to acting. But whatever way that career decides to show up, I am certain to recognize it because it will have all the qualities I listed that are most important to me.

The art gallery and frame shop only met 80% of this list which made for less than a satisfying situation. My salary never came close to half of my highest paying job and most likely never would have unless it was franchised — in which case autonomy would be severely threatened with reporting to the investors and other people that I would answer to on a larger scale. From the first day, I was very aware of how the confinement (now made longer by virtue of the fact I was putting in more hours for my business) affected me.

When we list the *qualities* we desire to see as part of our reinvention, it may surprisingly reveal that what we *think* we might like is something entirely different. That is fine. It does not mean that we can't do it, and it does not mean we can't have a satisfying career. But we will acquire neither if we are not completely clear on what really makes us tick.

This is an excellent time to really drill down and get in touch with what you want. And as you make your own *list of ten*, remember that for the list to work it requires *exactly* ten items. Ten allows enough criteria to make it well rounded and really think about what you want. At the same time it also limits the number of things to showcase, allowing you to focus on what is really important to you.

Just know that satisfaction only comes with 90% or

more. Anything less is settling. And you have come too far in the journey to settle now. So go ahead…name your ten. The results may surprise you.

Ten things which are most important for me to have in a
_____

1. _____

2. _____

3. _____

4. _____

5. _____

6. _____

7. _____

8. _____

9. _____

10. _____

# Chapter Fifteen

·҉·

## Now Playing ~ Your Authentic Self

*"Once she was a frightened child, seeking shelter where she could
She now has a different domicile and she likes the neighborhood,
From her secret garden she plans her design
without any will to harm or malign,
She is no great riddle you'll solve, simply more highly evolved than most..."
...from* That's Not Where She Lives, *song lyrics*
*- Adrianna Larkin -*

Here's a question for you: when seeking your authentic self, how do you know when you have found the real thing? Here's an answer: being authentic should make you *feel* freer. It might seem awkward at times — perhaps a little alien...but definitely freer *and* more expanded.

If you're not sensing that, the question you should be asking yourself is: what part of the old way of doing things have I brought forward and given a new name?

It's very easy to get wrapped up in the "how to" part and focus on "doing it right." The temptation is to assign some sort of ritual to the process. While there are some rituals — like meditation for example — that help us focus and get grounded, there are others that are just poor substitutes for what we left behind. And in reality they are simply an exchange of one set of fear-based beliefs for another set of the same kind.

All too often in the name of "spirituality" people condemn the trappings of organized religion; but those same folks who moved away from assigning their personal power to the external source of God, the church or clergy will readily hand over their power to Angels, rituals, and other symbols as they look to different external sources to offer the same salvation.

Don't get me wrong: I am not anti-religion, nor am I anti-new age Spirituality. But I think that we must make a careful distinction between being tied to practices that are self-grounding and empower us, as opposed to those that externalize our power as we look to those things to *save* us. Aside from any belief system that provides comfort and support, I will go so far as to say that you don't need to seek divinity outside of yourself *because you already have it.*

**You already are *divine*.**

And that should be what is revealed at the core after we peel off all the layers. I believe each person's divinity is what is *authentic* — and unique — for *them*.

A few months before the first draft of this book, I interviewed Dr. Eric Pearl, author of *The Reconnection* (Hay House, 2001) who was featured in the movie *The Living Matrix* (Greg Becker/Harry Massey, 2009). As he was sharing the story of his own metamorphosis from chiropractor to energy healer, he described how he sought information from other energy healers to better understand what was happening to him and why he could suddenly heal people in ways that had never occurred for him before.

In his interview as well as in his book he described the skepticism that he was met with because he did not subscribe to any specific belief or ritual. We laughed on air as he described the story of how each healer he consulted gave him some indication he wasn't "doing it right." He went on to say that depending on the energy healer he conferred with, each had a different process so that there was not even a vein of consistency to act as a benchmark for the rituals themselves.

In making light of this during our interview, one of the listeners in the chat room insisted that we were diminishing the processes of other healers. It was at this point I had to interject: I would never diminish the process that someone needs to ground, orient, guide or help focus their innate talents and energies — whether it is a conventional religion or something deemed "New Age."

I do, however, draw a clear line between something that focuses intent for the purpose of personal empowerment versus the reliance on a process that keeps them *living in fear* OR supports the belief that *there is no power without the process* (which is also fear).

When you believe you can only avoid disaster, accomplish what you want, or essentially function in the day to day if the Angels, tea leaves, or guides *give permission*, causing you to doubt your own feelings or worthiness, you have transferred your power to something else.

*We all have everything we need at any time to access possibility. Belief that we do not is simply programming that we received, offered by those who have more to gain by us giving up our power.*

If you acquire a strong *feeling* that you shouldn't go somewhere, then by all means listen to it. But if you have to dance around three times, bow at the sun, burn sage and say any number of Hail Marys before you know when is the best time to brush your teeth (or to convince yourself that your healing is effective), you've denied your own Higher Intelligence.

I had a recent experience that showed up on not just one occasion, but at three different times and with three different friends who commented that they did not wish to "name" an old boyfriend. By keeping him nameless and/or out of the conversation — even terming him "unmentionable" in one instance — it allowed them to retain their power and keep him distant with no ability to create harm.

I couldn't disagree more.

It is only in the face of those things that once diminished us that we understand how much or how little power we are giving away. Think about it...if you can still be harmed by the *mention* of someone's name, or a reference to an event, how much ability have you just assigned that thing to create distress? More importantly, how little have you dealt with that *feeling* that is still holding you prisoner?

Whether it's an old flame, an experience, a return to some place we thought we would never wish to visit again, we can only know that we have wrestled our demons if they can no longer instill fear in us. Then and only then can we be our authentic selves. In my mind then, our authenticity looks a little like a mathematical equation:

*Your Truth (minus) that which does not serve (equals) Authenticity.*

And just for the record: I have my own little ritual — just one of many *intention setters* — that I perform whenever my children or friends leave my home after visiting. I imagine a protective bubble in my mind's eye that surrounds the departing visitor upon leaving my house. This invisible shield lights their way and protects them from harm between my house and their return home. Started as something that I did when my son was a teenager, I noticed it *made me feel better*. (There is my root of reality.)

But by no means do I believe that my guests cannot return home safely if, as I have on rare occasion, forgotten to do this. It is just a fun and quiet little game for my own comfort.

And that brings home another point: as you embrace and accept the challenge to reinvent your life into what it can possibly be, *remember to have fun*. You have already done the drudgery affiliated with stuff you don't like, why go through all the newness and uncertainty to land right back where you started?

Somewhere along the line it became commonplace to think we need to suffer. There is a great chance for our root of reality to surface in asking: who made that rule? But what if in reality we were meant to feel good, elated — joyful even — and the "bad stuff" was only there to tell us we were off course?

As you grow to become more in touch with how you feel and what your reinvention looks like, it can feel like you are peeling off layers of what no longer serves. You may even wonder if you will ever get to the core.

There is a shortcut that will help get you there: it is called play. My friend Jacque Weiss is a staunch advocate of taking time to play (www.EnrichmentExpert.com). In her transformational brainstorming and enrichment sessions she offers her participants "recess" as a means of getting in touch with their creative process, which naturally accompanies the *feeling* of having fun. She knows that many of us—and women especially—have been so conditioned to attaching ourselves to a list of things to do, we have forgotten what fun feels like.

When is the last time you can recall that you did something you enjoyed, something that seemed really like YOU? If you are like most people who plan and fill every moment with activity and never get to the end of your to-do list, getting in touch with that thing that "lights you up" is as necessary as spending time with feelings that seem too strong to confront.

And here's the hidden treasure—the "joy" will make the "bad stuff" easier to deal with—here's why:

Do you remember when we talked about our bodies and our brains needing time to adapt to changes and growing new pathways? As we practice having fun and getting comfortable with that emotion, those same physical structures become the ones that process everything else. In short, the practice of having fun for its own sake is as necessary to dealing with past issues as it once again requires *feeling* over *thinking*.

This is the point in time where you need to be even more conscious of what serves you and what does not. And I'll repeat: anything you substitute for your current situation should feel expansive, joyful, and authentic to *you*. Which means it may be very different from what has been the reality for other people.

I experienced a lot of frustration in the early days of my growth and trying to make things happen. I *had* to make things happen in the corporate world and my own business, so I *should* be able to make things happen with the "right" process. (This is actually an example of what I referred to as the exchange of one fear-based system for another.)

Upon reading a book where the author would tell me to write down my desires and look at them daily, or visualize every detail of the experience and do *that* every day, I thought this must be it! This ritual had worked for *them* and so it had to work for *me*. It did not. I got so focused on the writing and visual creation of detail I forgot the *feeling*.

This, by the way, is the chapter where "feeling" starts to be stressed so much you may begin to think of it as yet another "f" word. (You'll get used to it after a while.)

I certainly advocate writing down your desires or doing visualization, *if that is the most effective process for you*. I found out by accident that my brain prefers a different game: "Now Playing at a Reality Near You." What works for me is to have a movie running in my head of what could *possibly* happen—and even *may* be happening in a parallel universe. I am both the lead character *and* a member of the audience, where I sit with anticipation and delight in the unfolding of all my desires. I write the script, I pick the props, I put in the characters I want to join me on this journey...then I just sit back and watch the show. Actually, I suppose that makes me the entire crew...director, producer, writer...and the possibilities of empowerment are endless.

Pay attention to the word *possibility*. It has surfaced before and will surface again on this journey, because without a doubt it is the great eraser of all blocked paths. With a wave of the possibility wand, all things are cast into the material.

It also takes all the pressure off to perform. I don't have to feel like I failed because I did not acquire my outcome in a specific time frame—*it was only a possibility to begin with* — and as a possibility it has the potential to show up at any time.

*If we understand our desired outcome as just one possibility, it allows us to have the necessary detachment, while experiencing the feeling of fulfillment. This process allows for our* **optimum** *outcome to show up in the way that best meets our needs.*

If this process does not light you up either, make up your own. That's right. You can do it. Is it a vision board with cut out images from a magazine that keeps your desires in the forefront? Is it renting a convertible for a day to give you the sense of driving one? *Play* with this. What *feels* best to you? Only you will know what sends bells and whistles to provide you with the most authentic joy and good feelings.

And good feeling is what it's all about.

Consistently applying this, or any process, is what makes it work. My meditation allows time to run the movie in my head, but only if I make time to meditate daily. Finding a process will inspire you to take appropriate action, which, it so happens, is the other part of consistency.

If all you do is dream about having the ideal mate or losing 40 pounds, but do nothing to change patterns that have not worked for you, odds are slight that anything is going to change. In my mental movies I pay close attention to the appropriate action my main character is taking. That is usually a clue for me to take action in my real life. If, in my movie, my authentic self is performing on a national stage, I see a conversation with a publicist...we talk about press kits we have sent out and the relationships she formed in my favor…how we applied ourselves to get to this precise place and moment. Then she pats me on the shoulder to say "break a leg, kid" — at which point I go out to give a house raising performance, of course.

As a testimony to how well this process works, it was after running this very same movie in my mind that I made a connection with a marketing expert in one of my networking groups while still at the shop. It turns out she had a heavy public relations background. We formed a friendship, and because of her skills I was able to put together a really solid press kit — something which had always been a great stumbling block for me no matter how much research I did before.

In keeping it fun, lighthearted, and enjoyable you can remove the barriers that do not contribute to those feelings because you are exchanging a process of *thought* for one of *feeling*. And as that happens, you are perfectly sowing the fertile field of possibility.

So this may be a good time to ask: can your authentic self come out to play? Don't *think* about it…

Just say "Yes!"

# Sacred Fire Boarding Pass

PERMISSION · GRANTED · TO · COME · ABOARD

Notes
_____
Journal Entries

# Chapter Sixteen

·ۣۣۜۜۜۜ۠ۤ·

## A Trip to Space Mountain

*"You would call me cynical, and that would be so typical*
*yet I've seen enough of you to know you're still the same,*
*You look for another chance, but you can save your advances now*
*'cause I'm not filling a void with an even emptier space."*
...*from* I Had It, *song lyrics*
*- Adrianna Larkin -*

There was a time when I justified my lack of organizational skills as a sort of organization in its own right. "I know it looks like a mess, but I know exactly where everything is…" In reality, the clutter provided a convenient excuse for what I had christened a lack of time to get and stay organized; even though on the occasion I could not find what I needed — and there was always at least *one* — I spent a lot more time in what would more closely resemble a search and destroy mission.

For many of us, keeping "things" offers a sort of insulation and a cocoon for our identity. There is a spiritual principle that a life already filled with material things has little room for growth or new experiences to come in. From a practical standpoint, the more "things" you have (especially the unused ones) the more things you have to take care of...and the less time – and space – you have to enjoy your life.

As you make choices about your psychological and spiritual systems that no longer serve you, take a look at the physical world as well. My friend and fellow radio host Joe Rumbolo (www.healingtheuniverse.com) is so fond of saying *"it's time to dump the junk."* For me, that means there is a physical process that accompanies the mental and spiritual side of our reinvention.

After all, a fire needs some room to grow.

Removing the clutter is one of the most visible ways you can transform the energy of your surroundings. It's tangible and offers immediate gratification. The goal is to retain what has utility and get rid of anything that does not.

As one who seems to have a much greater ability to create chaos than order it, I have stumbled across a few things that help. Here is how I learned to break it down.

1. Economy of scale: Take one area at a time. I usually start with one room. If that still seems overwhelming, start with one area of the one room, such as a chest of drawers or a desk. If cleaning is something you absolutely dread, start with something easy so you get the immediate benefit of seeing progress.

2. Follow the face of the clock: I have found it easiest to address whatever area I am choosing to work on in a clockwise fashion. It gives you a place to start and you can see progress as you go, compelling you to

continue. If you have more than one floor to address, take one floor at a time and work with that same clockwise approach. You'll stay a lot more focused and motivated if you see big blocks of space start to open up.

3. Two piles and a trash bag: It's great if you have an immediate place to put things away, but many times that is not the case. If you have yet to set up an organizational system for each area, begin with throwing out the trash. If possible, designate an area where what isn't trash lands in one of two piles: that for which you have immediate use (defined by anything you could possibly need in the next 30 days) and that which does not.

4. Invest in compartments: Spending money on organizers and storage materials is a good investment. But if finances are limited, it's not really an excuse for letting clutter rule the day. I have used shoe boxes, popcorn tins — even made drawer dividers out of smaller cardboard boxes. Dollar stores and resale shops offer great values on small baskets and other things that can be useful. Compartmentalizing my junk drawer in the kitchen turned out to be one of the best things I ever did as I no longer have to separate thumbtacks from spilled paper clips which would get tangled up with the rubber bands intertwined with spare keys. (You get the idea.)

5. Look hard at what's left: After you have the organizers in place, put the "immediate use items" in

these. They, after all, should have priority. When looking at the remaining pile, try to look at this as what is truly not needed. Ideally most of this will be donated to a charity or recycled in some way; but there may be "keepsakes" or things that we just cannot separate from our emotional attachment. Find a place (or a compartment) for those in the new system you just laid out — and if you cannot find a place for them to be safely tucked away, you may need to look at why you wish to keep them in the first place.

Helpful hint: in an area such as a basement or garage that may be designed for storage, a two-year rule is a good one to follow. If you haven't had use for an item in two years, you don't need it. If this is too radical to adopt at first, consider 5 years as a marker — it's still better than having something sit on the shelf unquestioned that has a decade of dust on it.

**Junk as People Too** ~ It can be a difficult and painful thing to acknowledge that people can clutter our life as much as things. Who are you keeping company with that no longer serves who you have become?

This is a tough one. So many times as we begin to grow and expand, gaining confidence and renewed joy in our lives, those who were once closest to us haven't found a way to do that for themselves or simply choose not to come along for the ride. For that reason, they may be very uncomfortable with our transformation — so much so in fact that they may consciously or even unconsciously sabotage it.

It may be slow and gradual or become suddenly apparent that the people we used to enjoy spending time with are no longer offering the same kind of relationship.

When this happens we often have to make choices for the company we choose to keep — especially if that company does not support our growth. It becomes necessary to put some space between your sacred fire and those who seem to be hooking the hose up to the hydrant.

In the case of a friend, business associate or acquaintance, the answer is fairly simple: don't seek to spend unnecessary time with that person. But what if the person who would like to see you remain "unchanged" is a member of your family or even your mate?

In the case of family — brothers, sisters, parents — you may find yourself putting more distance between visits. Ironically, as you start to grow in your own fulfillment and they remain in a different place altogether, they may wish to spend less time with you. The best space for you to be in is one of *acceptance*. They may never come around to understanding who you have become. But that's all right, because they have their own journey to travel.

I would challenge you to re-evaluate and change the status of just one of your relationships that is not serving you at the present time. If it is a marriage partner and you have been afraid to ask for their support or help, this would be a good place to start. If it's necessary to involve a third party in the form of a trusted counselor or minister, then by all means do so. If it is a toxic childhood friend who you have outgrown, maybe it's time you became "too busy" working on other things.

We often seek permission to be happy, yet we don't ask for help when it is needed. Asking for help is often the most responsible and committed thing you can do. Some things just require assistance, whether it's from a friend, a book, a therapist or your own sense of divine intelligence.

If you seem to be meeting some resistance with a

partner but have a good basis of communication, this is the first place to start.

My husband and I have completely different subsets of skills. While Mike tends to be detail oriented and methodical by nature, I have only isolated bursts of these activities — usually when I am fueled by some raging inferno of creativity. If I am — as an example — writing a book, my focus becomes nearly pinpoint and lasered (with one toe over the border of obsessive) as I am required to draw on every bit of talent I have for detail to analyze thought flow and composition necessary for a book to make any sense. The action becomes virtually consuming, and my interaction with him during these times is a lot less than usual.

Before undertaking this particular project, I initiated a conversation. I explained that for a limited period of time I might seem "distant" — that I would do my best to remain sensitive to his needs but I could just easily overlook them. I offered that he could share the times he needed my assistance or desired my company but I may or may not be readily available.

In short, I got the "buy in" from my partner to support my efforts.

If you do not have the communication — or the buy in — consider getting some help. Is there a minister, counselor, or other party whose neutrality represents an opinion that you can both accept?

As you do this, it may be revealed that whatever reinvention you are seeking may be aided by other steps or a different process than you had previously considered on your part. Be open to the thoughts and ideas presented that may be different but might work for both parties. A compromise of some sort may be needed for you to complete your goal, and if that is the case you would be wise to recognize and accept it if it is needed to take you both in the same direction.

The classic quote from Abraham Lincoln applies here: "A house divided against itself cannot stand." If you cannot get your partner's support, or compromise your own position, be prepared to surrender something — because one thing or the other will be going away. It may be the dream or it may be the mate. If you cannot bear for it to be the mate, your choice may be to surrender the dream before you have expended unnecessary energy.

Whatever you choose, avoid labeling your choice as "good" or "bad." Understand that, at this moment, it was the choice that served your truth and authentic self, and that is the responsible commitment that we all need to make.

In seeking to change just one relationship that doesn't support your growth, whether it's dumping an old boyfriend who is draining you, allowing more distance between a parent or sibling who doesn't get you, or working on your marriage to better gain the support you need, you have set the stage to make it easier to change all other relationships to your advantage. And here's the "sparkle and shine" that sometimes reveals itself later on with our deep cleaning:

*You may also be liberating those whom you release to find a new pattern of relating to people or things — other than the way they have come to rely upon with you.*

In my experience, and many experiences shared by others, the act of "cleaning house" makes room for new and wonderful contacts to come in to support what you are doing. They offer their own vision of your greatness — and will remind you of it often.

167

Whether you are removing the "junk" from your house or your relationships, the underlying thread is about what represents that *responsible commitment*. I offer pairing of these two words because as I came into my own awareness they seemed undeniably linked with one another.

In my own past, I had commitments to things and people whom I had no business being associated with. That was part of my growth process, but I would not call it responsible. At the same time, although I felt responsible for a lot of things, that responsibility waned depending on how I was feeling at any given moment—it could come and go depending on my ability to commit.

Responsible commitment—when it comes to dumping the junk or anything else—is what allows for the paradox of space to be created when we fill it with what truly serves our sacred fire. Simply put: it is another source of fuel to help our light shine more brightly.

So go ahead. Be brave. You *can* begin to tackle the mountain of things or people that will not support your mission—even if it is in the smallest of ways, in one area or one relationship.

It only looks like an uphill climb because you're standing at the bottom waiting to start your ascent. Truth be told, once you start you may enjoy the experience more than you can imagine. And the view from the top, or at any point along the way, will astound you.

It promises to be the ride of a lifetime.

# Chapter Seventeen

## Who's the Fairest of Them All?

*"Once there was an island, surrounded by a sea*
*with waves that formed a wall of darkness*
*and a spirit whose name was Me.*
*Then so deep within this darkness a light became renewed*
*with a flame that rose to bring the daylight*
*and was brought by only You."*
*...from* Only You, *song lyrics*
*- Adrianna Larkin -*

Shakti Gawain, author of *Living in the Light* (New World Library, 1998) was a pivotal force in helping me understand how the people and things in our lives mirror how we are treating ourselves. At the time that I was beginning to understand this, it seemed I had a disproportionate number of wicked stepmothers—all with one kind of poison apple or another.

Even after "cleaning house" and making the conscious choices to let certain relationships go, it didn't change the attitude of my customers or business associates. At the time it seemed that I had a rash of clients with whom I was locked into some sort of power struggle—and common themes began to appear, ones that would inevitably set the stage for me to emerge with "the short end of the stick". Only after amassing an impressive collection of short sticks did I finally process that this was largely due to the way I was treating myself.

It took a while before I learned that the people and things in our lives offer us our very own magic mirror. At the same time I was discovering a variety of stories of people who, after undergoing some sort of personal transformation, suddenly find that their relationships transform as well — even with people who treated them poorly in the past.

If you are running into the same types of conflict, and if you understand that changes are needed but aren't sure how to make them, I invite you to go back to the Love / Fear scale that measured our satisfaction and dissatisfaction …only this time let's use it to measure acceptance and judgment.

| Judgment | Acceptance |
| --- | --- |
| Fear | Love |

I once found myself in defense of a personal declaration that "judgment is the food which fear feeds on." The person who countered this felt it to be the other way around — that fear fed judgment.

I think you can make a case for both sides being correct, but I will stand by my original statement because it offers a certain amount of pragmatism. I don't think we ever rid ourselves of fear in the human experience, but we can become increasingly aware of our judgments and determine if those fears are serving our purpose or not.

How we judge other things and people — as well as how we feel we are being judged — can tell us a lot about the degree of self-love we have and point to the areas that need some work.

For instance, I went through a period in my business where it seemed like every time I turned around someone was demanding more and more. (Remember the start of my story?) Everything seemed stacked against me. I felt pulled apart and conflicted in so many areas, and after a while it even translated to physical symptoms.

I *judged* the source of my distress as suppliers who sent incorrect materials, village bureaucrats who had no idea what it took to run a small business, the state taxes that seemed to favor larger businesses over smaller ones, etc., etc…and while some version of these things were present in my world, it was my *judgments about them* that were the real source of my distress.

I have read a lot of material on self-love. I agree with most of it. There is wisdom in creating the affirmations—our brain does enjoy its repetition—and I have used this technique myself with a good deal of success. There is great benefit to taking care of our physical bodies, (another strategy) although I think a certain amount of self-love has to be present for us to do this in the first place.

Granting time for play, meditation, exchanging the negative self talk—when you become aware of it—for positive statements all offer their benefits, but again some degree of motivation must be present to access these things. It rather becomes like a paradox. We have to love ourselves already to a certain degree, before we can love ourselves still more.

I would like to suggest an alternate route to the acceptance end of the scale. I offer that in spite of whatever you begin to notice in the relationships around you, whatever seems to show up in your own personal mirror, that you *grant yourself permission* to have an experience. And not just any experience, but the one that you *want* to have.

In essence, that is what happened when I returned to writing music.

With the progression of our years it is common to become more and more "responsible" to our careers and people we care about (as we become less and less tuned into our own feelings—at least that's what I observed). For that reason, we often find ourselves granting permission to everyone *except* ourselves.

Granting ourselves permission is a gesture of self-acceptance which is the root of self-love and forgiveness. It is also necessary for a successful reinvention.

The biggest reason reinvention looks different for us at twenty-something as opposed to forty-something is because of who we believe we received that permission from. The permission came from *us*—it always does—but it is granted based on what we believe is justified by external sources. We do it as it is "required" for the next job, relationship, our children, or place that we have chosen to live. We do it readily and frequently, (which supports the point I made earlier: we have all been here before) but it is nearly always for *other* things and *other* people.

Later, almost as if we awoke from a sleeping spell that was decades long, we find ourselves where we are today: with a desire to do it for the only one that it ever should have been done for all along—ourselves—and with absolutely no clue of how to go about it. Suddenly we are staring at our own reflection like someone with amnesia: overall there is this sense of familiarity, but we have severe doubts about our abilities, questioning if we first must be *the fairest of them all* in order to have what we want.

Guess what? You already *are* that beautiful reflection.

Only your judgment made it seem otherwise.

And awareness of the judgment — a good mirror for the fear — is all that we need. We can then grant ourselves permission *in spite of how we have judged ourselves*. It is in fact necessary that we do, because when that happens we have already begun to move up the scale toward acceptance with no more effort than it took to pick up a mirror.

As you no doubt figured out, I like to put on my "parenting hat" (it matches my "experience bag" so very well). So what I'm about to say should not be all that surprising. There is a lot of information available about addressing our "inner child." Most times this concept is described as some version of our younger selves that remained wounded or ignored when we were small.

If you continue to struggle with granting permission to yourself, how about granting it to someone else who is quite close and quite dear to you: that same small child.

What would he or she like to do that might be waiting for your permission? _____

_____

_____

_____

_____

_____

_____

_____

_____

_____

_____

_____

Can you see yourself playing with that child in his or her chosen activity? What other things or support might you offer to help your child play this game better? _____

_____

_____

_____

_____

_____

_____

_____

_____

_____

_____

The more I act in the role of my own parent, granting "permission" for my own needs and desires *in spite of how worthy or justified it feels*, the more I have the sense of working the self-love thing from another angle. At times it seems a bit contrary to what I have read in many self-help books—to build yourself up and then take action. I'm not certain the "how" of it even really matters. For me it was a question of getting the magic I need to dodge the bony fingered bimbo trying to hand me tainted fruit. (You definitely want to avoid her. She has just one end game: to make sure you stay asleep.)

Ideally, we want to arrive at the acceptance of everything—especially the *possibility* (there's that word again)—that we might be perfect as we are. As we learn to accept more and more as part of the grand design of our lives, we acquire another vehicle to travel from our base of fear to crest at self-love.

If you feel you are already "granting permission" and things still are not changing to the degree you think they should, take another look in that mirror. It may show you that some conflict still exists, that you are still making your acceptance contingent upon being worthy. The permission we grant ourselves should be *unconditional* without "strings" — or short sticks — attached.

If we remain conflicted in any way, that conflict is going to be illustrated beautifully in all of our other relationships, our environment, and even in our bodies. That was in fact my own issue at the start of my story as I felt "put upon" by the forces of "everyone else." In reality I was having an internal war with what I wanted to do.

I wanted to plan events and focus on the creative side of the business, but felt that I was chained to all the other things that were so uninspiring and disconnected from the reason I wanted to have my own business in the first place. It was all these things with chains that lived at the top of every list, and not one of them seemed to match my stronger abilities (all kinds of judgments here).

Our great emergence comes with the ability to see the image that stares back at us, in whatever way it appears as completely perfect without any need for alteration — beautiful and radiant.

And if the image is one of you frazzled and conflicted, accept that as being perfect for you too as it is showing you where you are on the map.

Either scenario yields the same result — it means you truly are at the perfect point and the *fairest of them all* for what *you* are about to do: grant permission.

# Sacred Fire Boarding Pass

PERMISSION·GRANTED·TO·COME·ABOARD

Notes
_____
Journal Entries

# Chapter Eighteen

## Service with a Smile

*"But go laugh and go play in some part of the day,*
*take some time to help somebody else,*
*The world is your oyster and in every choice you make*
*always be true to yourself."*
*...from* Words of Wisdom, *song lyrics*
- Adrianna Larkin -

When we think of using our gifts to make the world a better place, there is often an illusion — that the benefits offered to the world by these talents have to be measurable by some standard of "goodness" in order to have real merit. If we knew without a doubt that our sacred fire contributed to the elimination of global hunger, the creation of world peace, and offered a cure for all disease, many of us would feel more justified in taking the time to invest in ourselves and do just that.

But what if your sacred fire is accounting? What if you are someone who sees beauty in numbers, can watch as they flow with their own language and rhythm, and you feel a great deal of satisfaction in creating a balance sheet and seeing it all come together? (As far reaching as this may seem, I know people like this.) What if you are already doing that? How does that contribute to the overall wealth of the world?

*Your sacred fire always serves to illuminate the world through the service it provides.*

I would challenge you to think of it this way: when we do what we like to do and we're very happy doing it, *we are always offering service.* I appreciate the accountant who can ease my pain by loving numbers and taking the time to prepare a balance sheet that is wonderful and accurate and clear. Because I can't. I *need* an accountant, but I don't want to be one!

If after reading through all of this you still find it easier to question the value of your innate gifts, go ahead. Question them—just don't let that keep you from putting them out there.

Once upon a time when I was in my early thirties, I was told that I would help more people with my music than I ever would as a nurse. I did question this—truthfully I didn't really even understand it—but as my story points out, there were a number of people who went out of their way to tell me what the music meant to them. Suddenly it doesn't seem so far-fetched. Especially in light of our current health care system that is becoming increasingly more impersonal as time goes by.

And if you are still having trouble calling into focus what it is you were put on this earth to do...

*Look at where your service takes you.* What are you hearing from others that might be a clue to the gift that you are supposed to share?

My friend Susan, who played a large part in my own story, had been told for years that she needed to operate in some capacity as a counselor or therapist. Her ability to express compassion, analyze, and reflect back to anyone — even after knowing them only a short time — seemed to be a genuine gift. She has amazing skill when it comes to helping people arrive at an effective solution to any problem that might present itself. This is her service — one, however, that she has only recently come to own.

At the same time my own shop was closing, Susan underwent her personal evolution. Very simply, she sold all of her equipment and ceased making films. I was stunned when she told me this was her plan, as I had always seen her as highly organized, knew she had produced a number of clever short films, and was extremely well versed in the art form.

I asked her what prompted this change of heart. She explained that while she did appreciate the craft of making films, it proved to be an enormous amount of work that was never offset by the enjoyment and fulfillment she kept thinking it would offer. In truth: it was always a struggle. At the same time she had gained the awareness that she *never* had to struggle with helping people arrive at a sense of their own value, and yet she gained enormous satisfaction from this.

Her resistance to a title that reflected anything related to the field of personal growth was born of her bad experience with therapists and counseling and as it was her natural ability, it always seemed "too easy." Teaching (as she had done prior to making films) had in fact been the next best thing.

In her chosen field of adult education her instruction always went beyond any course material she was presenting as she made herself available to offer additional "life lessons" for her students—many of whom had not had these before and were drawn to her ability to offer problem-solving skills that would help them address their life issues. This in fact had been more rewarding that teaching the course content.

Susan's own sacred fire burns brightly these days as she has fully embraced her innate gifts. She now assists others in finding self-love by releasing old patterns of negative programming. Through her business, *Tranquil Hearts™* (www.tranquilhearts.com), her clients learn the skills necessary to acquire inner peace as they embrace their own purpose for a fuller, richer life.

*Just as sacred fire illuminates the gift of service, the gift of service can illuminate your sacred fire.*

The communication of love in offering your talents as a service should not be diminished. It is in fact the way we best shine our own light revealing our greatness and core divinity. The love that is attached to offering assistance simply for its own sake, places you at the far end of Love in that Love / Fear continuum.

| Self-absorption | Service |
|---|---|
| Fear | Love |

In the realm of metaphysics there is a reference to love as offering the highest "vibration" or frequency. This is the basis for The Law of Attraction mentioned in so many spiritual resources, but most notably the movie, *The Secret*. The vibration that is highest will be the most magnetic, and if you are desiring to know what your service—or sacred fire—looks like and how to link with it, then consider becoming part of a volunteer effort or lending your skills to a special project, as this can be a great place to start. I am aware of countless stories of people who offered up help in one form or another simply because they had an idea or skill that was needed and bumped into their passion along the way.

So let's take a moment and look at the *science* of vibrational energy. Considering what has been published in the field of science about vibration in relation to matter, as well as the role played by vibration in spirituality, it could be that this is the most solid thread that connects what at one time appeared as oppositional forces. I am far from an expert in either field, but I think this is the right place to at least examine what I've been shown and have come to believe — because as we talk about loving service, we are really talking about the *power* created by the intense vibration that is formed from that love.

As one who considered herself a product of science (although I had dabbled in energy work for years), I had struggled with some of the earlier information I received from the spiritual realm. For instance, reincarnation was something that was possible, only since I personally could not prove that it was *not* possible.

We will always find a box shaped to hold our beliefs. When I would hear accounts of past lives or historically detailed accounts that were offered by someone who had been regressed under hypnosis, I considered genetic memories as a possible explanation that one might give for that amount of detail; although, in reality, I could find no more support for that theory than the past life experience.

Still resolute on the side of science, which I felt was necessary for me to remain impartial and objective (as if there really is such a thing), I came across some interesting information.

Upon reading accounts and research, I found things that rocked my world, like the reports of the same particle being in two different places at once, or that particle movement was altered just by a scientist observing it. What really blew me away was the report of a particle that could suddenly become a wave of energy, then return to being a particle again. My "objectivity" suddenly had a whole new flavor.

## A Case for String Theory

When I was in grade school, we were learning that the smallest unit of matter known to man was the atom. There were subatomic particles which we learned about called protons, neutrons, and electrons, but these were only parts of the smallest whole, again believed to be the atom.

By the time I got to college chemistry, I learned that there were particles of matter believed to be smaller than what I previously knew as subatomic particles of the atom. In fact, these provided the construction for the known protons and neutrons. Termed *elementary particles*, they had funny names like "quarks" and "leptons" and redefined what I understood to be building blocks of matter.

String theory gives credence to the belief that there is yet something smaller—and based on what I know, it substantiates a lot of what has been related to spiritually as the "Law of Attraction."

My venture into string theory was initiated by a repeating connection in several books I read that referenced vibrational energy. It used modern quantum physics—the same branch of study supported by respected scientists such as Albert Einstein, Niels Bohr, and David Bohm—to create a theory for what is believed to be the smallest unit of matter, best described as a vibrating string.

The premise for string theory as I am able to relay it, in my very limited basis of understanding, is this: even smaller than atoms, smaller than quarks and leptons—in fact THE smallest unit that is responsible for creating matter in the whole of the cosmos—is theorized to be a one-dimensional string that vibrates at varying speeds. As it does, it creates a magnetic field. The higher it vibrates, the higher the magnetic pull and the higher the attraction. All matter has these units in their smallest of particles, so all matter is energy that can *potentially* "create" as part of its existence.

In the context of science (as well as spirituality), the missing link to that creation—remember we said it could "potentially" create—and what causes those smallest units to vibrate at higher rates of speed is <u>consciousness</u>. The most prominent factor that tells us what *our* consciousness is creating at any moment then is: our *emotion,* or how we feel.

Hence my karate instructor's old saying, "You will find what you are looking for" holds true. It certainly gives another dimension to the power of positive—as well as negative—thinking, and why our feelings hold the key to our personal transformation.

**What's Love Got to Do With It?**

Love is obviously a very strong emotion. Reported as being one of the most common factors in unexpected recovery from a terminal illness, the consciousness of love (whether related to love of your home, love of your free time, love of your mate, or love of anything) is said to work miracles. So what could we do if all of our activities— *including our service*— were created from love? And what love could be created if we just offered our services that we may even take for granted as Susan did?

Everything that I have studied indicates we *vibrate* at a higher level with the emotion of love than we do with any of the other emotions—even fear.

So love given OR received as the result of anything we connect to creates such an enormous power in the vibration of physical matter that it can potentially take you places you might never have thought you could reach.

It can restore your health...or lead you to your sacred fire.

Have you ever had a really trying day where the smile of a friend, or even a stranger, made you feel better? What about the daisy chain offering from a five-year-old? And while you're still smiling at that one, there are a few more questions.

List the talents, skills, and abilities you have that seem "easy." _____

_____

_____

_____

_____

_____

_____

_____

_____

_____

_____

_____

How do you think these can be offered to benefit others? _____

_____
_____
_____
_____
_____
_____
_____
_____
_____
_____
_____

Still not sure? Recall the last five times someone complimented your abilities or thanked you for helping them—what were you doing?

_____
_____
_____
_____
_____
_____

Try a small experiment: the next time you find yourself in a moment of tension just stop, exhale, smile, *and think of someone or something you love.* The service you offer in changing this one aspect of your vibration may be the greatest gift you give—not only to yourself, but to someone you have yet to know.

# Sacred Fire Boarding Pass

PERMISSION · GRANTED · TO · COME · ABOARD

Notes
_____
Journal Entries

# Chapter Nineteen

## Ready, Aim, Surrender

*"A small voice inside that is calling, tells us what we need to know,*
*A balance that keeps us from falling so far*
*will take us where we want to go.*
*Love will be there..."*
*...from* Love Will Be There, *song lyrics*
*- Adrianna Larkin -*

All of my experiences in the traditional work world, from that of an emergency room nurse, to a corporate manager, to owning my own art and framing business required that I *get things done*. If I could anticipate what needed to be done down the road as the ninth, twelfth or fifteenth possible step—which I had the capability to do— then I always felt like I had the advantage. This made me a good fit for a fast-paced—and later—corporate environment.

However, this same skill failed to serve me as well when it came time to engage my sacred fire for performance. I knew how to promote myself, entertain my audience, and craft songs. I could easily transfer my knowledge of public speaking to the details of posture, diction, and voice projection when auditioning for a part or performance.

But with all those things at my disposal, there was still one very important part that was missing: *my ability to get out of my own head and enjoy the experience for what it was.* That is not to say that I *never* experienced that all-important present moment-ness that makes life so very sweet. But these times would come most often as gentle accidents.

In reality, they would have been much better appreciated in the context of *intention.*

It seems paradoxical to "intend" your surrender to the moment. But if you're not in the habit of loosening that grasp automatically, sometimes it's the only place you can start. The Buddhist teaching refers to this as "mindfulness" and it is the most powerful tool you can access for your own reinvention. Why? Because you are always noticing how you *feel at that moment.*

Often as I would go into a new venue and had no expectation, I began to play for myself. In doing so I noticed how much more engaged my audience was. As I enjoyed the experience with all of its magic and ability to connect me with my true inspired purpose, I noticed that others picked up on that intention as well. It had the additional advantage of minimizing my angst brought on by performing with an instrument, as my only focus was the joy of doing what I loved doing most: sharing a story in song.

I mentioned during my own account a pattern of "Defeat, Surrender, Return". If we revisit that for a moment, I can explain that the motivation behind having my second CD release at the Sheldon Concert Hall (with the experience of performing to eight people) was largely fed by the desire to be viewed as professional, and to offer testimony that I had reached a certain level.

This was, after all, my *second* CD; I could use it to my advantage to beef up a pretty lean press kit when soliciting for jobs locally or sending material to be published. And I don't know that it meant anything to anyone but me, but somehow I felt I needed the legitimacy offered by standing on the same stage once occupied by Arlo Guthrie and Janis Ian.

The glory of standing on that stage for its own sake — surrounded by its wealth of history, acoustic perfection, and tradition while in the company of two talented and supportive musicians — was lost in the detoured focus of how such a poorly attended concert would be viewed. The greater understanding that came about as the result of how that story unfolded, as well as everything I had gained from the experience, would not even be realized until many years later.

In that experience, it was only when I considered "all to be lost" with no expectation for a certain outcome, that I could arrive at that perfect space of enjoying the music for its own sake. It was *then and only then* that I could surrender to give what I knew to be the performance of my life. (Remember: in my mind it was going to be my last, so my only intention was to make it great.)

What was successfully accomplished in the experience of "defeat" was my complete surrender to the present moment without any attachment to outcome.

We don't have to know defeat if we utilize our intention to remain present in the moment. With intention, trust automatically joins in. Trust then becomes the other face of surrender. Oftentimes they are treated as two separate issues, but I've come to see them as different sides of the same coin. I don't think you can surrender intentionally without trust, and I don't think you can trust a process intentionally without having first surrendered your insecurities surrounding it.

If you have consciously surrendered to live in the perfection of the present moment, there is no concern about the future. That sort of angst cannot exist. The only possible explanation for that state is that trust is there along with the surrender. In the same token, if you have complete faith in an outcome, such as the ability to complete a report by a certain time frame, you are not experiencing the angst over how to get it done, you have already surrendered any doubt and trust is all that remains.

The point of surrender and trust is necessary to truly enjoy and revel in that complete present moment experience—in fact it guarantees it. If done completely, one process is all you have to master because the other one will soon follow.

Our sacred fire will always try to steer us to the present moment experience as this is where we form a link with our divine intelligence. Whenever we try to offer our gifts outside the presence of that living-in-the-moment joy, no matter what the intention—good or otherwise—the power of our sacred fire often creates the circumstances to force our surrender, flexing its muscles until we return to the present moment experience, where we should have been all along.

The process is very much like a kiln that has a cycle of heat to make clay a thing of solid form. Once it has completed its cycle, it temporarily subsides until it is needed again. We should not be surprised then if our sacred fire "flashes" to force our hand toward that perfect state of surrender.

For some this may appear as the loss of a job we really did not enjoy except for the security it offered. For others it is the separation from a partner who minimized our growth. For someone else it could be the loss of a home to force relocation to another setting that offers unexpected resources to support your growth. Using my own example, it was a concert where I had too much expectation attached to what I should look like, rather than what I could become.

Just weeks before writing this book and days before I was signed to the talent agency, I got a lesson in trust and surrender again. I was experiencing a sort of stall in my creativity. Rarely does that happen, but when it does I feel completely lost.

I could not write—music or anything else. I could not find work—neither within nor without the field of music. In fact, it was as if I did not even exist. That morning as I began my meditation, I returned to the Buddhist temple in my mind where I had gone to find so many answers before. As I was bent on getting them, I "stormed" the door and found myself face to face, once again, with myself.

"OK, we have all the answers, so tell me: WHAT THE HELL IS GOING ON? I've done my work, I can get on board with this whole financial meltdown that I get to have, but frankly, this sucks! I can't get any job performing music or doing anything else. My creativity is virtually non-existent. You have got to give me some answers because there is a limit on even what my "expanded" mind can endure. WHAT IS IT THAT I AM SUPPOSED TO DO?"

My higher self just laughed and offered two words:

"Accept *everything*."

"Everything?" I replied. I thought I had already done that. And it did not occur to me that I had left anything undone.

"Everything," she repeated. "Your inability to create, your fear involving that, your lack of work, your own greatness, the ten extra pounds you gained, your propensity for getting lost, your love of good coffee, your 'bizarre' sense of humor, the unsolicited support of good friends, and the pettiness of other people. Those things you consider to be blessings as well as those things you consider curses: *EVERYTHING.*"

And I suddenly understood that this was a test of mastery that revealed to me that I had some work yet to do.

As I have moved forward from that day, I do my best to remember that my intention has been consciously directed to take aim at everything I wanted. I have readied myself as well as I can. The only thing that I am still reminded to do: *is to throw up my hands in surrender.*

When I do, the rest will take care of itself.

# Chapter Twenty

## Our Final Frontier

*"With joy that gives rise to the wave that is waiting in me*
*to reach out and speak out to teach and to grow*
*to remember to love and believe...*
*The test that each of us takes lies not in our darkness but in our own grace,*
*to face the challenge in dawn of every new day*
*and remember to say Thank You..."*
*...from* Thank You, *song lyrics*
*- Adrianna Larkin -*

Having arrived at our *acceptance* of current events, the next challenge is to give thanks for them.

The benefit of offering gratitude for any situation, regardless of what that situation looks like, is consistently emphasized in self-help, metaphysical, and spiritual teachings. From these perspectives, feeling gratitude is akin to feeling love — which we already know to be essential in raising our vibration and drawing more of what we want into our reality. In short: our appreciation appreciates — *or grows* — the value of all that we consider *good* in our lives.

It is understandably difficult that we find it hard to give thanks for a failed business venture, a poor health outcome, or any other absence or tragedy that's challenging to face. We are after all human, and it seems contrary to our very being to be gratified by hardship. As someone in the midst of a loss right now, I know that some days my husband and I think we are doing well just to function in this setting, let alone remember to be grateful for it. In a perfectly enlightened state, however, we would all be able to do that automatically—express our gratitude and allow this experience to be illuminated by our sacred fire.

The propagation of certain pine trees is actually aided by the devastation of forest fires—the intense heat of the fire causing the cones to open, the seeds to be released, and the germination process to begin. I remember traveling throughout parts of the west and seeing charred landscapes with a feeling of sadness that so much was lost. But that was before I knew that the intensity of heat and destruction was the catalyst for creation, starting the new growth needed to keep the landscape intact. Without it, the landscape becomes stagnant and would die anyway.

My mother used to say, "There's an end to every era." As I've grown older, I better understand her wistfulness as a metaphor for our own mortality. It doesn't have to be that way. Not if we recognize the space that remains as something that holds the promise of new life.

Nature has a way of naturally filling any void that is created. (Hence the pine cone analogy.) If there is nothing you can see that is serving as the replacement for that thing that you have left behind, trust that it is indeed filled by the *space* created when it left. The truth is that another car cannot come into an already occupied parking spot. The space itself will remain to hold the spot when the car is ready for it, however.

The challenge then becomes offering thanks—not for

all the "undesirable" things that you may be experiencing — but for your own final frontier: the space and all the possibility that lives there.

A rose-colored-glasses viewing of all that "once was" only serves to feed our resentment at the departure. But if we focus on the arrival *instead* of departure, we join with our eagerness to greet what fills that void in whatever way it shows up.

In my own situation, I cannot help but feel a twinge of sadness when I go by the retail site where my shop once was. I had high hopes and many dreams, but in reality I don't miss the stress. I can remember lighter moments, the shared humor, the gratitude expressed by my clients. I can be grateful that I had this transition out of my corporate environment with a career that fueled my creativity.

At this time however, I am also grateful for a more relaxed holiday season, as we are not married to the 16-hour days that would regularly become part of our holiday "celebration." That experience always left my husband and me drained of anything that would have been left to enjoy our own festivities with family and friends.

Christmas would come and it was all I could do to remember to put money in a card for each of our kids. Forget shopping, forget decorating, forget anything else that I once enjoyed as the trappings of the season. As I complete this chapter it is nearing the end of November, and Mike and I actually decorated the house — inside and out. I will have the opportunity to handwrite Christmas cards; and I have even purchased some small token gifts to reacquaint myself with that sense of joy in giving a present that is unexpected and can be unwrapped. I *am* grateful that I can have this experience. It will be the last one of its kind in *this* house…and even knowing that makes it so much sweeter.

At the same time, rather than making that a melancholy thought, I imagine what our next home will look like. It could be smaller (we don't have three children living with us as we once did.) I have a chance to live in another part of the country, take in a new landscape — perhaps tour without a permanent home.

Anything *is* possible.

All that you are, all that you have become, every experience you have had has brought you to this point. Space is the great field of possibility (there's that word again). Remember when you bought your first new car, your first home, landed the first great job? What happened to that initial sense of elation and where did it go as you replaced it with the next new item of its kind, or the one after that? At the time you had those things you were in the moment, but that moment was recreated with a change that would follow.

This is just another kind of change.

The only difference between then and now is that in the previous example you perceived a conscious choice of selecting what replaced the thing you were willing to give up, and you knew exactly what that replacement looked like. I would pose another thought. It is possible you still do know what the replacement "looks like" and you will find it much easier to bring it into focus by giving thanks to the space that is held for it.

Regardless of your ability to do this, understand that *at all times* we are choosing what we want to replace that "loss" with to fill the newly acquired space in our lives. We can fill it with anger, fear, resentment, grief, and too much activity as we "explore" any number of things that place limits on our ability to move forward. Or we can go forward and fill it with surrender, trust, love, new opportunities, gratitude, and the light of our very own sacred fire.

The choice of our journey's end and final destination...has always been ours to make.

As I put the final touches on this chapter, I am reminded to share with you the visit from my own ego that competed for the space I was attempting to fill with my own possibilities. It managed to return after everything I learned, only to remind me of the importance of remaining in my own truth.

As I joined with the notion of placing this journey in a book form, my ego—with a history of self-talk, little of which had been positive in the past—showed up to repeat an old pattern...

*Ego: (dressed in a onesie and dragging a blanket) "What makes you think you can write a book?"*

*Response: "I've just started the introduction, let's see what happens."*

*Ego: "So I repeat—what makes you think you can write a book? Just because you have an introduction doesn't make you a writer, you know."*

I tune him out, as even loving mothers are occasionally known to do, and keep writing as I offer to put ego to bed and tell him a bedtime story. This works for a while until the little guy has a nightmare and once again pads out of bed. Occasionally he sees fit to wake me up in the middle of the night, but in my waking hours I keep writing. I must trust this activity as an expression of inspired purpose because the discomfort of not doing it is greater than doing it—and louder than the voice of ego.

*Ego (intensified): "So you really think you can write a book? There's more to it than that, you know. You have to find a publishing source, get it to market. What good does it do to write a book if no one can read it..."*

*Response: "Quiet now, I'm on the third chapter. I'm telling my story. It's all good, you can go back to sleep."*

*Ego: "No one wants to hear your story. You sound like a whiny little girl—or worse, a neurotic mess. What makes you think your story's so great?"*

*Response: "My story just gives the backdrop for the big picture. All the authors I have enjoyed or learned from made themselves vulnerable by gifting the reader with a glimpse of their personal side."*

*Ego: "So you think you're one of them?"*

*Response: "No, I think I'm one of me."*

*Ego: "Huh?"*

I almost had him there for a minute. But he was relentless, and he rallied.

*Ego: "Amazing. You still think you can write a book."*

*Response: "BE QUIET!"*

I actually woke myself up. I woke Mike up too, talking in my sleep in response to a dream I was having about this little kid screaming incessant taunts in my ear and getting on my last reserve nerve.

The next day I continue writing. I am now getting into the important part, focusing on the 11 steps that brought about my own metamorphosis and their application to reinvention.

*Ego: "What are you doing? Writing again? You can't be serious. You gotta' be tired of that by now. Writing a book is hard work. At least when you were working on your own story that was kinda fun, but you really don't know anything, you just think you do. Nothing you have written is going to help anyone."*

*Response: "Go to sleep."*

I am making steady progress. Chapter 15 is complete, followed soon by Chapter 16...then Chapter 17.

*Ego: "What makes you think you can write a book?"*

*Response: "I just finished Chapter 19, and thanks to you and your "inspiration" I decided to give you top billing in Chapter 20."*

Ego likes that. I imagine his eyes going wide at the remark, surprised, yet so typically immersed in his own importance. Unfortunately not enough so to silence his constant prattle; but I am now ready to face my accuser who repeats the question, just in case I have not heard it the many times before.

*Ego: "So. What makes you think you can write a book?"*

As I prepare to save my work on the computer and print the first draft, I turn to the place where—in my mind—this little guy would be standing, to look him in the eye and offer the words that finally made themselves appropriate:

*Response: "It's done. And now I have a question: What makes you think that I can't?"*

As I hold the completed manuscript in my hand, there is silence from ego. You can't argue with a finished product. I know without a doubt that it was my sacred fire that made this possible—in spite of every insecurity, limitation, and voice of ego.

That is the power and fury cast by the light of this intense flame: it illuminates for all—even the voice of our own ego—what otherwise could not be seen.

# Chapter Twenty-one

## The End of the Beginning

*"Make a difference, what does it mean?*
*When I look at you you're looking back at me.*
*Where's the logic, guess who gets betrayed,*
*just ourselves if we think we haven't made...*
*We make a difference."*
*...from* The Difference, *song lyrics*
*- Adrianna Larkin -*

This is as far as I go with you...the rest of the journey is yours to complete on your own. This has always been the case, but hopefully from this point on your climb doesn't seem as steep as when we first began. Believe it or not, you are halfway up the hill (and far from over it).

If I have done my job, you can now be a little more comfortable with being uncomfortable. That is all that is needed to take you the rest of the way. It is also completely possible that you find yourself validated in some way and are experiencing some degree of comfort for the very first time. That's alright too.

The last few chapters were intended to provide some

humor along with the more serious perspectives on the 11 things I consider universal to personal and spiritual growth. But just a reminder before I go:

1.  **Acknowledging your feelings** to help you expand intuition ~ Awareness of how you feel will be valuable in helping to distinguish between the voice of ego and the guidance of intuition. *Your feelings are the truest compass you own.*

2.  **Awakening to rebirth** to begin allowing for what is possible ~ You can pick any point as the place of re-entry and leave the door open for infinite possibilities. *You really are as perfect for the experience as the experience is for you.*

3.  **Observe and understand** how much programming you have received and how you can change that program — especially in the area of worthiness — to have what you want. Minimizing or discounting your desire for an experience is an aspect of feeling unworthy. *You are a child of The Divine and therefore* **always** *worthy.*

4.  **Truth** as it defines what holds value in your experience ~ We begin to understand that things "go away" to make room for what we *really* want. What should begin to fill that space then are things and people who align with our desires *regardless of the value assigned by others.*

5.  **Courage** to embrace change has a physical component. Listing the 10 things that you consider

most important in life, work, partnership or any area that you wish to change will keep you focused. Just know: *it will take some time for your body to adjust and make what is uncomfortable begin to feel normal.*

6. **Authenticity** feels expansive and is, for each one of us, something different. Your feelings will guide you and it will seem more like play than work. If it does start to feel like work, *consider that you may be holding onto old behavior patterns or beliefs and are attempting to apply them to the new life you are trying to make.*

7. **Responsible commitment** is the commitment we make to our sacred fire. It shows up as the space we make in our relationships and physical surroundings that nurture and support our dreams. It requires that we ask for help and support when necessary, and *if faced with a choice between two strong but seemingly oppositional desires, we trust whatever choice we make to be the right one for us at this time.*

8. **Self-love and forgiveness** is demonstrated when we grant ourselves permission to be just as we are, free from judgment about what might be lacking or how we look to the outside world. *It includes understanding that anytime you feel judged it is a reflection of how you are judging yourself.*

9. **Loving service** is offered to the world when we are doing what we feel inspired to do. We are an energetic universe that responds to vibration and the strongest vibration we have to offer is love. *The greatest and most powerful service we can perform for*

*the world then is to do what we love.*

10. **Surrender and trust** are served by intentionally placing them into our reality. If this is not natural for you, and if it seems that you are still having difficulty, look at what you may resist accepting. *Our ability to surrender and trust is gained only after we fully accept all aspects of our circumstances.*

11. **Gratitude** expressed for what shows up as a loss is not necessary as much as giving thanks for the space created by that "loss." *This one act is a complete expression of love and trust as it offers full access to all possibilities.*

If there is anything that still remains to keep you from seeing your greatness, I would ask you to look at who or what you might be blaming for that feeling. Do you now blame your parents? The government? Your spouse? The corporation to which you gave your loyalty for so many years? The church...

Just as we so often make our own prisons, we are equally accountable for the key. And as someone who has lived in that prison, I would invite you to consider that *you* not only hold the key, *but actually created that experience as being perfect for what you wanted to have in this lifetime.*

For many years I blamed my dad for "pushing" me into nursing and short-circuiting my career in the performing arts. When he died, I was convinced that there must be some kind of purgatory for people who suck the life out of another's dreams, boxing them into positions so far removed from their original intent — choices that they would never have made on their own.

The plain truth of the matter was that I couldn't see any way out of working in the hospital at the time and I was angry with what I assumed was my "lot in life."

A few more years would pass — many, in fact — before I gained a vital piece of information — and that something *more* that I could not understand with all of my study and inquiry. It was the final piece afforded to me only after the business had closed its doors in the summer of 2009. It was the single piece of information which would later serve to be the genesis of this book.

What I came to know is that everything had gone according to plan. Nothing had been "kept" from me, and all was set up as a contract which I agreed to before being born. All of the delays, detours, side journeys and business closure were those things I made and planned in order to bring me to this final moment. I was standing at the fork in the road, but it was only because of all that had happened that I could find myself here at this juncture with such a tremendous opportunity.

I had made a choice to delay my own engagement with sacred fire for the purpose of maximizing the return on that investment. My father, my mother, prior spouses — even those affected by my actions in ways I wished I could undo — were all just playing the supporting roles that they agreed to take on before we came into physical existence.

I was about to embark on a wonderful journey, which — if embraced fully — would be the thrill of a lifetime and could make that "love" connection for myself and so many others in the most remarkable of ways. I could be a force for hope and healing. I could facilitate the paths of others to increase the amount of love in their lives, growing that energy exponentially as they shared their sacred fire with a world so hungry for it.

I suspect that there are many like me — waiting and delaying gratification to make the experience that much sweeter. It is now our time. We live in a world that has become so desperate for a loving touch. Each of us has a contribution to make and that contribution plays an integral part in healing our planet.

If we ever had the luxury of considering ourselves separate and individual from all other life forms, our own technology (which has done equally as much to create barriers) is showing us that we are an ever-shrinking globe with interdependence on each other — as well as the climate and our plant and animal kingdom.

One breath, one event, one cosmic or seismic shift changes the face of our world in the blink of an eye. From the start of editing this book until its completion, I watched as the country of Haiti — essentially unchanged for decades — had its topography and people changed forever in an earthquake that claimed hundreds of thousands of lives.

In gestures that demonstrated unlimited capacity for compassion, countries and communities rallied support for their global neighbors, for people whose names or faces remain unknown to them, just as they have through the last decade of great catastrophes — both manmade and natural — to reveal their potential for a tidal force that can heal *worlds*.

But to date, disaster is the only consistently unifying force. We seem to need the reminder of our own mortality and vulnerability in order to express our greatness. We have a pattern of showing our light only in the face of great loss.

As we are awakened by devastation we are soon lulled to sleep again in the return to "normalcy." What once defined a great tragedy registers only briefly as a change to the New York skyline, a differently defined shoreline following a tsunami or the rebuilding of a southern city from a flood that spared its historical French Quarter.

Some would say that events which cause mass destruction and loss of life are cosmic wake-up calls. I'm not certain there is value in accepting or disputing that belief. History reveals that both natural and manmade disasters have occurred throughout the ages; but never in our history have we had the tools available as we have today to join hands and demonstrate our ability to help and heal. There *is* a better way to come together—one that trumps the reminder of our need to do so by a time of crisis.

It is by *choice* then, and not default, that we are meant to come together in these most remarkable of times. Only then can we illuminate our own divinity to recognize what would be too easy to overlook: igniting our own sacred fire.

*Now understanding your purpose,*
*the sleeper awakens within*
*Allowing your greatness to surface,*
*for the journey that you must begin*
*For each one of us has been chosen,*
*to become what we know as Divine*
*But how many more remain frozen,*
*waiting until they can find, their*

*Sacred Fire*
*At the center of the flame*
*Something higher*
*You know is calling out your name…*

# Sacred Fire Boarding Pass

PERMISSION · GRANTED · TO · COME · ABOARD

Notes
_____
Journal Entries

To the reader:

I've so much enjoyed having you as a traveling companion—and I hope it helped to know that there was an entire convoy of us keeping you company as you made your way through these days. On the chance that I sparked a growing interest and you'd like to read further on some of these same subjects, I am including a list of the books, movies, and websites that offered valuable information and proved helpful for my own journey. They may offer some insights to your own. There are, of course, a vast number of significant resources and materials to choose from beyond those I have listed here. I encourage you to seek and find answers that have personal meaning for you, but always keep in mind:

This is your journey…remember to enjoy the view.

**Books:**

Atwood, Janet Bray and Chris Attwood, *The Passion Test~The Effortless Path to Discovering Your Destiny,* Hudson Street Press, 2007.
Breathnach, Sarah Ban, *Something More~Excavating Your Authentic Self,* Warner Books, Inc., 1998.
Canfield, Jack, *The Success Principles, How to Get from Where You Are to Where You Want to Be,* Harper Collins Publishers, Inc., 2005.
Choquette, Sonia, *Your Heart's Desire, Instructions for Creating the Life You Really Want,* Three Rivers Press, 1997.

Diaz, Al, *The Titus Concept, Money for My Best and Highest Good*, Morgan James Publishing, LLC, 2005.

Dyer, Dr. Wayne, *Change Your Thoughts — Change Your Life*, Hay House, Inc., 2009.

Gawain, Shakti, *Living in the Light, A Guide to Personal and Planetary Transformation*, Nataraj Publishing/New World Library, 1998.

Greene, Brian, *The Elegant Universe*, Vintage Books, 2000.

Hay, Louise, *You Can Heal Your Life*, Hay House, Inc., 1984.

Hicks, Esther & Jerry Hicks, *The Amazing Power of Deliberate Intent, Living the Art of Allowing*, Hay House, Inc., 2006.

————*The Astonishing Power of Emotions, Let Your Feelings Be Your Guide*, Hay House, Inc., 2007.

————*Ask and It Is Given, Learning to Manifest Your Desires*, Hay House, Inc., 2004.

————*The Law of Attraction, The Basics of The Teachings of Abraham*, Hay House, Inc., 2006.

————*Money and The Law of Attraction; Learning to Attract Wealth, Health & Happiness*, Hay House, Inc., 2008.

————*The Vortex, Where the Law of Attraction Assembles All Cooperative Relationships*, Hay House, 2009.

Lipton, Dr. Bruce, Ph.D, *The Biology of Belief, Unleashing the Power of Consciousness, Matter & Miracles*, Mountain of Love/Elite Books, 2005.

McTaggart, Lynn, *The Field, The Quest for the Secret Force of the Universe*, Harper Collins Publishers, 2001.

Puryear, Herbert B., Ph.D., *The Edgar Cayce Primer, Discovering the Path to Self-Transformation*, Bantam Books, 1982.

Roman, Sanaya, *Living with Joy, Keys to Personal Power & Spiritual Transformation*, H. J. Kramer, Inc. Publishers, 1982.

————*Personal Power through Awareness,* H. J. Kramer, Inc. Publishers, 1986.

————*Spiritual Growth, Being Your Higher Self,* H. J. Kramer Inc., Publishers, 1989.

Roman, Sanaya & Duane Packer, *Creating Money, Keys to Abundance,* H. J. Kramer, Inc. Publishers, 1987.

Scheinfeld, Robert, *Busting Loose from the Money Game, Mind-Blowing Strategies for Changing the Rules of a Game You Can't Win,* John Wiley & Sons, Inc., 2006.

Shimoff, Marci with Carol Kline, *Happy for No Reason, 7 Steps to Being Happy from the Inside Out,* Free Press/Simon & Schuster, Inc., 2008.

Tolle, Eckhart, *A New Earth, Awakening to Your Life's Purpose,* Penguin Books, 2005.

————*The Power of Now,* Namaste Publishing and New World Library, 1999.

Twist, Lynn, *The Soul of Money, Transforming Your Relationship with Money and Life,* W. W. Norton & Company, Inc., 2003.

Tzu, Lao, *Tao Te Ching,* translation by Man-Ho Kwok, Martin Palmer, Jay Ramsay, Barnes & Noble Books, 1994.

Walsch, Neale Donald, *Conversations with God,* Hampton Roads Publishing, 1995.

Zukav, Gary, *The Dancing Wu Li Masters,* Perennial Classics, 2001.

**Movies:**

What the Bleep Do We Know!? (2004)
The Secret (2006)
The Living Matrix (2009)

**Websites:**

www.maryrobinsonreynolds.com ~ supplies valuable information on Masterminding as well as coursework and other resources to facilitate the process.

www.tranquilhearts.com ~ recommends method and practice of meditation as listed on the blog. For some, meditation can seem intimidating at first, but this site provides helpful material to assist you in making meditation a regular part of your day.

www.thepassiontest.com ~ offers an alternative to the "List of 10." The passion test is another assessment tool you can use to uncover and identify what you really feel passionate about.

www.jnunziata.com ~ presents information and coursework to help you fine tune your purpose and remove blocks.

www.EnrichmentExpert.com ~ a unique, playful combination of an enrichment and power brainstorming process called "Recess"™, which offers problem solving through creative possibilities.

# About the Author

Adrianna Larkin is the professional name of a Midwest-based singer-songwriter, recording artist, radio show host, and author—all of whom answer to the name of Nan. After spending most of her adult life as an octahedron in a round hole, (her words) she launched a full-time entertainment career writing and performing *conscious music* in the summer of 2009, following the close of her family business. An unintentional renaissance woman, she has held a variety of jobs—working as a waitress, shoe model, emergency room nurse, piano tuner's apprentice, stay-at-home mom, real estate agent, corporate manager, and retail entrepreneur. It was music, however, that remained present in some form through all of her evolutions.

In addition to a full-time career performing music, she contributes her talents to acting and voiceover work. Every Tuesday at 7:00 p.m. Central she serves as host of ***Passion's Purpose & Prosperity*** on BlogTalkRadio.com— a radio program featuring nationally and internationally known guests who offer their tools for reinvention and the engagement of a passionate life. She adds, "I think it's important that we each recognize our own divinity...this is what is needed to heal ourselves and others. It allows us to make the passionate choices that lead us to our true purpose, growing the sacred fire."

She is always eager to hear the reinvention stories of others. If you would like to share yours or inquire about booking Ms. Larkin for a speaking or performance engagement, please visit www.adriannalarkin.com.

Ms. Larkin resides in Southwestern Illinois with her husband and two furry assistants, "acting coach" Sadie the cat and "assistant radio producer" Josie—a border collie and lab mix who offers her expertise on content, copy, and production, all from the comfort of the living room couch.

Igniting the Sacred Fire

www.ingramcontent.com/pod-product-compliance
Lightning Source LLC
Chambersburg PA
CBHW031247090426
42742CB00007B/343